UNHOLY MATRIMONY

UNHOLY MATRIMONY

The case for abolishing marriage

Liz Hodgkinson

COLUMBUS BOOKS

Copyright © 1988 Liz Hodgkinson

First published in Great Britain in 1988 by
Columbus Books Limited
19-23 Ludgate Hill, London EC4M 7PD

British Library Cataloguing in Publication Data
Hodgkinson, Liz
   Unholy matrimony: the case for abolishing marriage
   1. Marriage
   I. Title
   306.8'1
   ISBN 0-86287-421-1

Printed and bound by Mackeys of Chatham Limited

Contents

1	The confusion that is marriage	9
2	Marriage today	21
3	Marriage through the ages	47
4	The tyranny of togetherness	73
5	Why marriage is bad for women	91
6	Why marriage is bad for men	117
7	Marriage, money and the law	139
8	So what about the children?	157
9	The ritualization of marriage	181
10	Credo	195
	Bibliography	203
	Index	205

Acknowledgements

The writing of this book has been made possible by the existence of the wonderful Fawcett Library, now housed in the City of London Polytechnic, and its equally wonderful and helpful staff. My greatest thanks go to them, but I have had valuable assistance from other excellent organizations, including the National Council for One-Parent Families; Mediation in Divorce (Richmond branch); The Equal Opportunities Commission; The National Marriage Guidance Council, now called Relate; and the International Wages for Housework Campaign.

1
The confusion that is marriage

The proposal at the heart of this book is one that some will perceive as revolutionary and many will find disturbing: it proclaims that marriage is an anachronism, a practice no longer relevant to our society, and that the institution should be legally abolished.

But why? Marriage is surely very much a part of the fabric of our society and, indeed, of every community in the world since time began. Almost every adult marries at some time or another, and the event would seem to be as much a part of human existence as being born and dying. We talk of 'births, marriages and deaths' in the same breath, and we are given certificates for attaining each of these milestones on the road of human existence.

Why, then, as marriage seems so normal and natural, should I claim that it is out of date and ought to be abolished?

Marriage, in the terminology of this book, denotes the state institution which, at the moment, fundamentally alters the legal status of men and women and binds them to each other virtually for life.

It is, however, very much open to question whether the institution of marriage in itself has the power to foster or encourage any of these positive aspects of human relationships – friendship, love, commitment, companionship, familial devotion, for example. Although marriage is generally supposed to increase people's happiness and encourage men and women to behave well towards each other, it frequently has the opposite effect. All too often, people who have got married in the belief that marriages are made in heaven find themselves living in something that more closely resembles hell. The divorce rate, world-wide, is higher than it has been at any time in history. There are more broken homes than ever before. At present almost as many people walk out of marriages as walk into them. According to the Office of Population, Census and Surveys in London, there were, in 1984 (latest year for which figures are available), 396,000 marriages and 158,000 divorces (figures provided by the Mediation in Divorce Conciliation Service) in the UK: a more than one-in-three failure rate. We expect a lot of marriage – but we rarely ask whether the institution can live up to our expectations. Yet marriage is still very popular; the vast majority of the world's population marries, often more than once.

This is not to say that happy marriages do not exist. Many couples enjoy living together and have very good relationships – but this is likely to be *in spite* of their being married, not because they are legally bound to each other by a state institution. It is not the laws and conventions of marriage that have brought them happiness, but the fact that the couple has a close rapport, communication and understanding between them. Such a relationship, a 'marriage of true minds', does not depend on a couple's ability to conform to the strictures of a state institution.

Most of us long for a fulfilling relationship, a union in which there is perfect love, perfect companionship and perfect compatibility. The exceptions who want to go through life alone prove the rule. But the institution of marriage does not insure against loneliness and isolation, nor does it guarantee love, happiness or sexual satisfaction. The only guarantee that marriage offers is that once the register is signed the parties are henceforth legally tied to each other, no longer free to act as single people, and that the knot will be quite difficult to untie.

Is marriage primarily a legal contract, in fact, or is it mainly a private commitment between two people? Do we get married, nowadays, because we are in love and want to bind ourselves permanently to one special person? Is the overwhelming justification for marriage having children and raising a family? Do we marry mainly because we want to acquire a permanent sexual partner? Do we do so because we imagine that being married will make us happier than being single? Or do we enter into wedlock simply because it is expected of us and we will be thought odd if we don't?

Nobody really knows. Although there are many laws governing what married people may or may not do, no marital expert could say with certainty what marriage is really 'for' today. The qualifications for marriage are however clearly defined: partners must be either single, widowed or divorced, and of opposite sexes; they must not be close blood relatives; and there is normally a minimum age stipulation as well. Some countries recognize polygamous marriages, but nowhere in the world is marriage between two people of the same sex legally valid.

First and foremost, then, marriage is a union of two people of opposite sexes. As this law is so universal, the main purpose of the institution would seem to be that of reproduction, and in the past this was certainly the case. The whole idea of marriage was to 'increase and multiply'. This concept is enshrined in the Church of England marriage service, which was formulated in the sixteenth century. The marriage service has never been holy writ: it was devised by politicians after the Reformation. Although it may have acquired a spiritual patina over the years, it is not the revealed word of God, but a man-made text directing a man-made procedure.

Marriages of four hundred years ago were rarely embarked on out of the partners' love for each other. They were contracted to ensure the continuity of a legitimate line, to consolidate powerful families, to produce descendants. In peasant and lower-class families, children were needed to work on the land, or to help out with the animals and do other household chores. In those days reproduction was the main reason for people marrying, because marriage ostensibly ensured that children were brought up in homes by both parents.

Nowadays, however, many people who marry do not want to have children. They take every precaution they can to ensure that reproduction does not take place. Are they, then, legally married? Are people who do not want children entitled to marry? Can a couple who are over the age of reproduction legally marry?

Unholy Matrimony

The answer to all these questions is 'yes'. Although marriage may have originally been intended for reproduction, ever-increasing numbers of people now marry without any such intention. Yet their marriages are perfectly valid. A man who is impotent can contract a legal marriage, as can an infertile woman. Neither party is compelled to undergo a fertility test as proof of his/her suitability as a marriage partner.

If people no longer marry primarily because they want children, do they then marry because they want to have a permanent sexual relationship? Yes, according to the marriage service. The concept is indeed enforceable by law. Although you cannot legally compel people to reproduce, and failure to reproduce is not normally considered grounds for divorce, it is perfectly possible to end a marriage if sexual relations do not take place.

This raises the first anomaly: you cannot compel people to have children – the fundamental and primary purpose of marriage – and yet you can compel them to have sexual intercourse with each other. A marriage in which the sexual act has never taken place is considered to be unconsummated and may therefore be annulled. A relationship in which one of the parties has consistently refused the other sexual intercourse may also be dissolved. Yet those who abstain by mutual consent continue to be legally married, if they so wish.

In the past, it was often very difficult for unmarried people to have sexual intercourse. Until as recently as the 1950s society considered sex to be something that belonged within the context of marriage, and that ideally no one should perform the sexual act outside this institution. Sex and marriage were deemed to be inextricably intertwined. The Church preached that sex was, above all, one of the pleasures of marriage, and morally wrong outside that institution.

But today sex and marriage are no longer considered to be inseparable. In the West, almost nobody who gets married is a virgin: the vast majority of brides and bridegrooms have previously had more than one sexual partner. Extra-marital affairs are nowadays commonplace, even though the idea of the

The confusion that is marriage

'open' marriage seems largely to have gone out of fashion. Even the Church has its own small share of what used to be called 'fornicators' – and of practising homosexuals. Homosexuals are not at present allowed to marry each other, yet a majority of people now believe that they should be allowed to express their sexuality openly.

Where, then, does this leave marriage, given that it is neither the bastion of legalized procreation nor the sole socially acceptable context for sexual relationships?

The question of sex is itself problematic. Most of us grow up nowadays with the notion that sex is something desirable and personally fulfilling, something which adds pleasure to life. This idea is a very recent one. Although sex has no doubt always been a very powerful drive, in the past it was often considered more of a duty than a pleasure, an act of shame rather than one to be celebrated. Married people engaged in sex because they had a duty to reproduce. If they enjoyed the exercise, that was an added bonus – but it was certainly not its primary object. We now tend to believe that if we are not sexually 'fulfilled' within marriage, we have every right to seek such satisfaction elsewhere, or to find another partner who will please us more.

A potent reason why people marry is for companionship, or mutual support. But although many people would cite companionship and compatibility as prime ingredients of a happy marriage, these factors are certainly not a prerequisite. People can legally marry if they hate each other, if they are complete strangers, or even if they have never seen each other before. This is common, of course, in the East, where arranged marriages are still the norm. Even Benazir Bhutto of Pakistan, who was educated in the West and is in many ways a very liberated woman, opted for an arranged marriage to a man she hardly knew. This marriage may very well turn out to be companionate, but one could hardly say the partners were already close companions. Nor were they at all in love. How could they be? They had only met a few times before the wedding.

We in the West tend to regard such arranged marriages as barbaric and primitive, forgetting that it is only in the past hundred years or so that most Westerners have been theoretically free to choose their marriage partners. In property-owning classes, and especially in royal and aristocratic circles, marriages were very often arranged for dynastic purposes or for reasons connected with inheritance. The marriage of Prince Charles and Lady Diana Spencer was, however one likes to look at it, practically 'arranged'. His bride had to be suitable, which meant she had to be not only single, but a virgin, of the Protestant faith, and from the right social background. Neither party had to be in love, or even companionable, for the marriage to be legally valid, but it *was* considered essential that the Windsor line should be continued.

The evidence is, in any case, that being in love can be a very bad basis for marriage. Many such unions quickly founder when the romantic haze dissipates and the partners have to face the day-to-day reality of living with each other. Once married, people often find that they have very little in common, and that their initial attraction does not provide a secure enough foundation for a long-term partnership.

Marriages of convenience are of course legally valid. A marriage to somebody who is a citizen of another country may be contracted in order to gain citizenship or right of entry into that country: officialdom may have been opposed to such marriages in recent years, but it can be very difficult to prove that a certain couple married only for the purpose of nationality or for rights of residence or employment. Marriage has always been, and still is, a time-honoured way of getting out of a country one wishes to leave. Many Polish girls, for instance, go to Britain and America as *au pairs* or nannies in the hope that they will meet a boy they can marry, so that they will have the right to live outside their native country; and immigration that would otherwise have been illegal often becomes legal after marriage, because marriage changes legal status.

In no sense can the marriage vows guarantee that the parties will actually love and honour – let alone, in the bride's case, obey – or that they will forsake all others thereafter. Nor can the vows ensure that the couple will become happier and more contented

The confusion that is marriage

once they are married. The institution of marriage does not have the power to convey any positive improvement to people's lives. But what marriage *does* do is alter people's legal status, forever.

Divorce does not necessarily end a marriage, as divorced people often find to their cost. A couple that has been married can continue to make claims on each other, especially financial ones, long after the decree absolute has been granted. It is possible for people to sue ex-husbands or, less usually, wives for maintenance many years after the divorce has been finalized. Indeed, some people are advised by their lawyers to continue making maintenance claims in case the ex-husband or wife should come into some money, so that they can claim a share of it. Once divorced, the parties no longer have the right of sexual access, and they must normally live apart – but they may still be tied by children, or by alimony regulations.

So how does marriage alter legal status? In Britain, and in those countries which have in essence adopted the British model of marriage – that is, Canada, the USA, Australia, New Zealand and South Africa – there are no actual 'laws of marriage' on the statute books. Nevertheless, successive marriage and divorce acts as well as individual court cases have established a large body of legislation governing marriage.

Modern marriage is based, above all, on the notion of 'one flesh', interdependence, and the idea that the parties will be a team rather than separately-operating individuals. When we sign the marriage register, we enter into a legally binding contract. The problem is that because there is no actual print, small or otherwise, no rubric covering rights and duties, most of us have little idea what we are committing ourselves to; we learn only gradually. We may make 'vows', but usually we do not know how far these will be binding. If we promise to 'obey' and then don't obey, are we committing a legal offence? If we promise to love and honour, and cease to do so, are we falling foul of the law?

The first time married people are confronted with marriage laws is normally when something goes wrong and they want to end the marriage.

Hence our confusion. The marriage service says one thing, the marriage acts say quite another, and our own inclinations probably tell us something else.

My main quarrel with marriage, and the overwhelming reason why I feel it should be legally abolished, is the concept of 'one flesh': the idea that by becoming married people stop being independently-acting individuals and become an inseparable unit.

My other objection is that although marriage alters the legal status of both men and women, it does not alter this status in the same way. The laws relating to marriage assume that the man is the breadwinner and the woman is his dependant. Once a woman marries, she in fact relinquishes many rights – even though she may not realize it at the time.

Her income, for instance, will be considered part of her husband's for tax purposes, and the tax forms will be addressed to him. It is possible, of course, for married couples to have their tax separately assessed, but they have to make special arrangements for this. It does not happen automatically. Also, a married woman's unearned income must be declared on her husband's tax form even when the couple has opted for separate assessment. She has no financial privacy. Yet there is no corresponding duty for a husband to reveal any private income to his wife. On marriage, the man gains the married man's allowance, but there is no corresponding married woman's allowance for the wife. This long-standing anomaly is due to be rectified (in Britain) in the 1990s. But perhaps the greatest anomaly of all is that non-earning married women normally have no financial independence whatever.

A married woman is assumed to be kept by her husband, whether she wishes this or not or whether this is in fact the case. This means, in practice, that she cannot claim supplementary benefit or family income supplement on her own behalf. As yet, the laws governing financial arrangements do not recognize that married women can be financially independent. Many feminists have argued against marriage, claiming that it is a patriarchal institution that benefits men and oppresses women. This cannot be denied. The only 'line' that is considered to be worth preserving is the male line, the only name worth having the male name. In the past women with illegitimate children often married to give their children a 'name' – that is, a man's name. Their own names were not considered good enough to pass on.

Even if no children had resulted from the union, a single woman who was known to have slept with a man was regarded as soiled goods – though if the man deigned to marry her he could thereby make of her an 'honest' woman, as if the formality of marriage cleansed the relationship. Strangely, no single man who had sexual relationships with women was ever regarded as sullied; he would be as good a 'catch' as any for his eventual bride.

I believe that marriage has always disbenefited women, and still does. The notion that, within marriage, women become lesser partners is enshrined in the custom of changing the woman's name to that of her husband. Though this is *only* a custom, not a legal requirement, it underlines how totally women can disappear in marriage. Many women also continue the custom of calling themselves 'Mrs John Smith', thus annihilating themselves.

I also believe that there is no way to make marriage fair and equitable to both parties. It is just not possible to have marriage laws that will suit all circumstances. Marriage will always turn two people into, at best, one-and-a-half people. And you do not have to be a radical feminist to realize that the 'half' is usually the woman.

Britain's iniquitous taxation and property laws have encouraged ever more people to opt for living together instead of being legally married. As they see it, this enables them to gain all the advantages of companionship, friendship and intimacy without submitting themselves to the penalties of marriage.

Those who support the idea of marriage may say that the laws are there to protect the weaker party – that is, the woman. It is very much open to question, however, whether these laws *do* offer much protection. There is no law that can compel a man to share his property or salary with his wife, though a spouse may find that in the event of a break-up he/she has some claim to a proportion of the value of the matrimonial home. Half of the husband's income

Unholy Matrimony

is not automatically the wife's. Nor can any law compel a man to treat his wife well, to love her, to look after the children or to provide a cosy, clean, well-furnished home.

Conversely, no law can compel a wife to love her husband, to have his best interests at heart or to be a good companion.

Embedded in the divorce laws, however, is a statement to the effect that each spouse has a right to the other's consortium – that is, to live together as husband and wife. The trouble is that there is no precise definition of what this means – no statute setting out the rights and duties of each partner. But there *is* a legal right, implicit in the laws of marriage, to sexual intercourse; rape within marriage is not as yet an offence in Britain unless there has been a previous court order forbidding cohabitation. (Such an offence does exist in Scottish law, but only in cases where the couple are legally separated.)

The law also assumes that married couples will live together in the same home, although they cannot be compelled to do so: again, this is implicit in the divorce laws (not doing so constitutes separation and therefore, after a suitable time has elapsed, grounds for divorce). But no woman who wants to live apart from her husband can be compelled to return to him, or *vice versa*. None the less, separate homes do not in themselves mean that the marriage is at an end. Indeed, in recent years some perfectly happily married couples have chosen to live in different homes. Sometimes this arrangement takes the place of daily long-distance commuting, and couples get together mainly at weekends. In other cases, and comparatively rare ones, geography is not a factor: the writers Margaret Drabble and Michael Holroyd live apart, in separate establishments, even though they are recently and happily married. However, the upkeep of two separate homes invariably costs more than that of a single matrimonial dwelling.

As married people are still assumed in law to be a team, they cannot be compelled to give evidence against each other in a court of law. (Until the Civil Evidence Act of 1968 a wife could not be compelled to testify against her husband – hence the criminal Pinkie's sudden decision to marry his girlfriend in Graham Greene's novel *Brighton Rock*.) Generally speaking, in law and in everyday life a husband and wife are deemed to have a duty to support each other, and to be loyal, even if one of them has committed a crime.

Marriage was originally ordained not in heaven but very much on ground-level: to protect property rights. The laws governing the property interests of married people are still far stronger, and very much more enforceable, than the rather vague ones relating to friendship or companionship. This means today that if a house is purchased in the name of one spouse only, the other will have an interest in that property. (The Married Women's Property Act of 1882 made it possible for married women, as opposed to spinsters and widows, to own property.) In addition, the non-owning spouse has a right to occupy the matrimonial home, and to remain in this home even after the death of the owner. The Matrimonial Homes Act of 1967 gives the non-owning spouse a right of occupation provided he or she has contributed to the value or management of the household, or helped the spouse to do his/her job, or brought up children. Either spouse may apply to the court for enforcement of that right.

The matrimonial home is supposed to be a haven, the ideal environment for the friendship and companionship of marriage. In practice, of course, this is often not the case. Women who are married to violent men may find that the matrimonial home is the least safe place on earth. Yet in law the man has a right, especially if he pays the rent or mortgage, to occupy this home, however he behaves. The woman may have nowhere else to go – and no personal income, if she has given up her job to look after him or bring up children. Women who do this are frequently described as 'housewives', as if they were married to the matrimonial home, but if the husband gives his wife a housekeeping allowance out of his income, no portion of this automatically becomes hers, as any other housekeeper would expect. Moreover, any property purchased out of savings from the housekeeping allowance will be considered to belong to both spouses. Housekeeping cannot be considered 'escape money'.

The law also states that marriage invalidates all previously-made wills. A married person cannot leave money exactly to whom or what he or she likes and be sure that his/her wishes will be honoured. For instance, if a married person says in a will, 'I leave all my money to such-and-such a cats' home', it may well transpire that the surviving spouse has a stronger claim.

The laws applying to money, property and wills are currently in a state of flux, indicative of the fact that nobody knows any more what marriage should or should not be: a private arrangement between two people, or an institution that is subject to state laws. Politicians, marriage guidance counsellors, priests and lawyers are currently addressing themselves to the matter. All realize that the present situation is unsatisfactory, if only because there are so many divorces and so many problems cropping up within marriage. Most thinking people accept that the present marriage laws need a comprehensive overhaul.

My own proposal, to be outlined in the course of this book, is that the state institution of marriage should be replaced by legally executed contracts tailored to suit the individuals concerned. This will allow a wide variety of relationships, and also permit flexibility of content. If marriage is considered to be a contract, it should be subject to the same strictures as any other contract: it should be renewable at set stages and able to be ended or altered without hostility or acrimony between the parties. Such contracts would allow people who wanted to form intimate relationships to make provision for property, children and disposal of income. But there would no longer be a blanket law which applied to everybody, whether it fitted their circumstances or not.

I firmly believe that all men and women should be legally single for the whole of their adult lives, and that personal relationships they may happen to wish to form should not affect their legal status. The idea that married people are interdependent, one flesh or an indivisible team would be replaced by the assumption that all men and women are independent, autonomous and able to look after themselves.

It is a radical idea – but one which I think is eminently workable.

2
Marriage today

Modern marriage is in a bad way. Although couples may agree to love, honour and share all worldly goods at the outset, few of them stick to these vows for any length of time. Many couples end up hating and resenting each other, even resorting, in extreme cases, to violence and murder.

The condition of being married and having to live in close and intimate contact, day after day, year after year, with just one adult member of the opposite sex, encourages very strong dependencies to develop. Married people expect, and are expected, to share general interests and political persuasions, to take an active involvement in each other's work and hobbies, and to go on holiday together. Such cosy togetherness is constantly encouraged by society. Many of us get married, or form partnerships, assuming that this familiarity will make us happy, content and fulfilled. Indeed, in modern Western marriages it is almost impossible for partners to get away from each other for any length of time. Married people are expected to sleep together, in the same bed, and to live as much of their lives as is humanly possible as a unit rather than as individuals. The idea of joint mortgages and joint bank accounts, hardly heard of twenty years ago, is regarded as a good idea, and the concept of joint finances underlines the way in which we like modern couples to operate.

In the old days, and also in marriages in traditional societies, men and women did not, and do not, spend so much time together. In many traditional societies today (Muslim ones, for example), it is usual for husbands and wives to entertain separately, to eat separately and to have completely separate tasks. It has been said that this separation occurs in societies where women are kept down, but in her book *Sex and Destiny* Germaine Greer makes the wise point that it at least allows the wives a bit of a breather on occasion, time away from the spouse. It has long been received wisdom that Western marriages allow more freedom to the wife, who does not always have to be at her husband's beck and call. If this is deemed to be good, why should it be so desirable for two disparate human beings, of different sexes and possibly of quite dissimilar characters, to share everything they do?

Nowadays, we insist on shared parenthood, shared housework – even shared secrets (openness of feelings, thoughts and emotions). Men and women sometimes also dress alike, particularly if they are sporty types. Advertisements aimed at retired or soon-to-retire people reveal an assumption that, once the couple are no longer in paid employment, they will want to spend every single minute in each other's company. No wonder people who stay married for a long time end up looking alike. (There is some scientific credence for this: according to the psychologist Robert Zajonc of the University of Michigan it happens because married people mirror each other's expressions and behaviour, meeting scowls with scowls and smiles with smiles.)

Modern marriage can be stifling, because it makes it so difficult for partners to spend any time away from each other. And however much a couple may be in love when they first meet, however strong the initial 'urge to merge', in time they will most probably want to reassert their individuality. But if they start out with the idea of being mutually dependent, unable to stand on their own feet, they may actually in time be incapable of doing even the simplest tasks alone. What the psychologists call 'learned helplessness' is common in marriage, and the condition is liable to worsen as the years go by. Many women who have been adventurous and independent while single discover that, once they have been married a few years, they are nervous about changing a light-bulb, booking into a hotel alone, or making decisions about even a minor purchase. Men who have been coping excellently as bachelors suddenly forget how to cook, to sew on buttons, change bed linen or how to send trousers to the dry-cleaners.

But the more a couple merge as the years go by, the more we see this as a good thing. Kitty Muggeridge, wife of the journalist Malcolm, once admitted in an interview that over the many years of their marriage they had become 'one person'. We also have a sneaking admiration for couples who involve themselves in suicide pacts, as did the writer Arthur Koestler and his wife Cynthia, who decided she could not live without him. 'Greater love hath no woman [or man] than this,' we reflect. Yet the fact is that people do not really become more alike over the years. If anything, their differences become more apparent as the years go by. And in those marriages where they seem to have merged, what has really happened is that one partner has allowed his or her personality to become *submerged* by the greater force of the other. Where couples do appear to become 'one flesh' it will not be a case of two separate, strong individuals making a whole that is greater than the sum of the parts: instead, one person will have effectively died, become a cipher, an incomplete human being. In many cases – although not all – it is the wife who allows her personality and individuality to be sucked dry and taken over by the stronger (or more aggressive) personality of the husband.

Nowadays, we seem desperate to tidy people up into couples, so that they will move in society as a team, a unit. We forget that humans are not really designed to be parcelled up in this way. One of the main reasons why marriage tends to bring out so many violent emotions in people is because they are resisting – often without being fully aware of it – being imprisoned for life with just one other person. It is now very common for married women to become clinically depressed. Depression is really anger turned inwards. Husbands tend to turn their anger outwards, and become aggressive, demanding and bad-tempered, blaming everybody apart from themselves for what has upset them. Often, neither partner realizes that he or she is silently rebelling against the straitjacket of marriage, the institution that was supposed to make them so wonderfully happy. Many partners try to escape by having affairs – but all realize that, once married, they are in a cage from which they can never really escape. At most, they go for short sorties, but their wings have been clipped. Even people who divorce usually get married again quite soon. We are so indoctrinated into marriage that few of us can envisage a life without total symbiotic union with another human being.

Again, in the days of the extended family, there was always somebody of one's own sex to talk to, and with whom burdens could be shared. Nowadays, most women have only their husbands to talk to, most men only their wives. There is a general idea that, once married, a couple should be left alone, to sink or swim together. In-laws do not want to 'interfere', and they would rather not know if anything is going wrong. No wonder there are so many marital problems, infidelities and divorces. The institution has become stifling, yet it is constantly presented as the only way to live, the only way to relate to another human being, the only way to love. If you love somebody, so the current wisdom goes, you must want to bind them to you, permanently if possible. This bondage is usually, euphemistically, called 'commitment'.

There is little freedom in the context of marriage. Togetherness is encouraged both on an everyday social level, on which husbands and wives who do not function as couples are deemed to be a problem, and now, increasingly, in a business context: spouses are often expected to attend office parties and similar occasions, and even, if the employer is a sizeable corporation, to go along on business conferences attended by their partners (a big business is growing up in the arrangement of 'spouses' programmes' at such junkets). And for all our talk of sexual freedom, we do not, as a society, condone sexual intercourse outside marriage. It is acceptable for single people to have as many partners as they like – or at least, it was all right before the advent of AIDS – but once married, men and women are expected to be able to channel their sexual urges into their marital partnership. Society very severely castigates anybody who strays, or rather, is caught straying.

Our current fantasy is that marriage partners should be able to satisfy each other sexually, and that neither should look around for somebody more exciting, newer, younger, unless divorce or widowhood has intervened. This concept of so-called 'serial monogamy', now generally accepted, entails getting rid of the current partner before embarking on a liaison with another.

But society still reserves its severest criticism for those who are caught having affairs with other people while they are still married. This is 'cheating', or 'being unfaithful', and those in high public office or with an otherwise high profile cannot normally escape the indignation of press-generated public opinion. For public servants, the penalty for being found out is a duty to resign immediately from their high position, and there is a general understanding that such people will have to atone in some way for what they have done, because they have broken the rules.

This happened in 1983 to the MP Cecil Parkinson, after he was discovered to be having an affair with his secretary Sara Keays. Many of us were not quite sure whether to blame Parkinson for cheating on his wife, or Sara Keays for going along with the affair knowing that he was a married man with a family. But we all felt that Parkinson had been doing something unacceptable.

The number of well-known men in public life who have had to atone, often for years on end, for having sexual liaisons outside their marriages, is legion: Gary Hart, the 1988 American presidential candidate; John Profumo, who has spent many years working among the deprived of London's East End since his adultery with Christine Keeler was discovered in 1963; and Lord Lambton, who went to live abroad after he too was discovered, in the early 1970s, to be having an affair with a prostitute. It is less often the case that women in high office have to step down because they are having a secret affair, but then very few women are ever in high office. Throughout history, however, the penalties for women 'caught in adultery' have been severe. One can only wonder at the level of shock and horror that would result if it were to be discovered that Mrs Thatcher or the Queen, for instance, had secretly been having affairs while in positions of authority and trust.

Marriage carries with it the notion that sexual fidelity, 'belonging' to each other, is important. This notion has never been more highly upheld than it is now, in the late twentieth century. In the eighteenth century, when marriage was regarded more lightly, both husbands and wives often had lovers and mistresses, and not always in great secrecy. In medieval times, marriage and love were almost completely separated. One married for duty and fell in love for pleasure – but rarely did one fall in love with a marriage partner. If one was lucky, fondness and respect might develop over the years spent together.

Now, as the song has it, love and marriage go together like a horse and carriage. Once we marry, we are expected to be in love with that person forever. But if we fall in love with somebody else, it is all right for us to get divorced and marry that person. However, woe betide any man and woman who choose to live together just as friends, or as brother and sister. They would be regarded as distinctly odd. A conviction prevails that it is part of nature's plan for us to be permanently united, sexually, financially and emotionally, with just one other person. Many of us believe this is what God ordained for us.

The case of the millionaire novelist Jeffrey Archer in 1987 confirmed our entrenched views of the married state. Archer felt that he had to clear his name when newspapers alleged that he had paid money to Monica Coghlan, a prostitute, to prevent her revealing the nature of their relationship. In the event, it will be remembered, Archer cleared his name, thus making himself £500,000 the richer (he gave the money to a variety of deserving causes).

Archer's case had a curious effect on the British public, and encouraged many people to analyse exactly what they thought marriage was all about. Each day throughout the hearing his wife Mary, at that time a Cambridge don, was loyally by his side, quietly and smartly dressed. Both found themselves bathed in a plethora of publicity.

The facts of their marriage, so far as they have been made public, are these: Jeffrey and Mary Archer married in 1966, when she was 21 and he was 27. Both were Oxford graduates, heading for glittering careers. It says much for their perception of the importance of the ceremony that they had their wedding videoed, and kept a video-recording of it, part of which has subsequently

Marriage today

been seen by millions on BBC television. Jeffrey Archer, a compact, ever-smiling, confident young man, went on to become a Conservative MP and was also a keen runner. He resigned his seat when a bad business deal bankrupted him, but rapidly restored his fortunes by writing bestselling fiction.

Mary, meanwhile, though she stayed in the background, was not just a wife and mother. She continued a career of her own, as a scientist and university lecturer. As time went on, the Archers prospered mightily, had two sons and became pillars of the Church. Mary was shown on television playing the organ and singing in the choir. Jeffrey was depicted as a devoted father, and shortly after the court case had his first play successfully premièred in London.

But the main focus for the media throughout the period of the libel hearing was on the Archers' marriage. How far could they be considered the ideal modern couple? It appeared that they had everything – money, looks, a family, wonderful homes, domestic staff – and, wonder of wonders, total devotion to each other after 21 years together. Mary has a career, is good-looking, well-dressed, neat, confident. Both, indeed, are very confident. They obliged for the cameras by being photographed hand in hand, arm in arm, the archetypal modern couple, both earning, both successful, both high-profile, and both with very nice things to say about each other. 'Mary is completely honest,' said Jeffrey in his most sincere manner. 'She is the most honest person I know.'

So the story became 'How to stay married, Archer-style'. Mary and Jeffrey became instant experts on marriage and their views were sought in interview after interview. When asked how she made her marriage 'work', Mary Archer replied that she didn't rate strict sexual fidelity that highly, but thought it was important for couples to be loyal, and able to stand by each other. That statement alone made many journalists reach for their word processors. 'Do you agree that sexual fidelity is not a top priority for marriage?' asked the *Daily Express* of its readers. The columnist Helen Mason wrote in *The Daily Telegraph* that Mary Archer was 'stuck in the 'sixties' to give low priority to sexual fidelity. 'We have seen the alternative to sexual fidelity and it does not work,' Mason wrote. 'Rejection of concepts such as jealousy and possessiveness sounded very noble, but in fact, cleaving unto the other only, as we all promised to do, has a sound practical value.'

Helen Mason went on to say what she thought that 'sound practical value' was, and as one might expect, fear of AIDS came top of the list. Security and trust were also mentioned.

Mary Archer was also widely castigated for saying publicly that she did not think it was possible to be 'in love' after 21 years of marriage, though she declared that she was able to love her husband dearly. This called forth the wrath of newspaper columnists, in particular Lynda Lee-Potter of the *Daily Mail*, who said she was not sure Mrs Archer was right in saying that it was impossible to be in love after many years. She asked her readers to disprove this with their own stories and, of course, they obliged in droves, saying that their husbands/wives brought them flowers, presents, declared their love, that they never spent a minute apart and missed each other deeply and inconsolably if one was absent for any length of time. What passed for being 'in love' was, of course, over-attachment and dependence, and not real love. Though we may very much enjoy spending time in the other's company, surely true love means being able to let the other person go, never wanting to bind him or her to you. Wanting to bind a person to you comes from fear, not love.

We try to maintain the fantasy that being in love is a good thing, and that passion and excitement in marriage are also a good thing. In saying that she did not believe it was possible to be in love after many years, and that strict sexual fidelity was not of prime importance, Mary Archer was simply being honest – one of her greatest qualities, as we heard from her husband himself. But honesty would now seem to be a rare commodity where marriage is concerned.

All of us conspire to keep alive the fiction that marriage works, that closeness and commitment are of paramount importance. If we were to admit what marriage is *really* like, it would be revealed as an emperor without clothes, a cloying, confining and repressive union which has the power to imprison at least one, if not both, partners. Modern marriage is, I believe, largely a pretence – a hollow state that we all pretend to like because most of us cannot envisage any other way to live. Society now moves in couples and will exclude us, we believe, if we dare to move alone. The fiction is that, so long as we have a partner, all will be well. Even if that partner causes us more anguish than happiness, it is still better, we believe, to have somebody to whom we are joined by law than to be alone.

The 'ideal' for marriage is in fact a continuing honeymoon. At this stage, although the partners may be sexy and passionate with each other, they are not allowed to be sexy with anybody else. They are also supposed to have the other's interests at heart all the time, to stay in love, to prove this with presents and acknowledgement of anniversaries, and to become mutually dependent on each other. They are not supposed to want to look elsewhere for intellectual, emotional, sexual or any other kind of personal satisfaction, but are supposed to find all they are looking for in this other partner. We seem to feel that men and women are, by themselves, incomplete and can only be 'completed' by attaching themselves permanently to a member of the opposite sex.

Even gays and lesbians are now aping the married state, and are increasingly forming lifelong liaisons of a marital type. Some homosexual couples are even getting 'married' or, rather, having their unions blessed in church. The whole world, it seems, must get married. Anybody who does not do so is considered slightly odd, somewhat eccentric, or even unlovable, and is likely to be put under pressure by his or her peers to form such a liaison.

Married people are supposed to support each other and be devoted to one another. They are not supposed to grow apart or develop their own personalities. People do, of course, all the time, but as a society we do our best to encourage the idea that, once married, a couple are welded together for all time.

The supposition is that total togetherness is a highly desirable, indeed enviable, condition. Autonomy is out.

From time to time, reports and surveys about marriage appear in the newspapers. The surveys always prove that there is still overwhelming support for the institution, and as a subject marriage fascinates everybody, not least because there is such a huge disparity between the fantasy and the reality.

There is also a widespread belief that marriage is now treated too lightly by many couples. In one survey about 75 per cent of adults interviewed felt that the institution ought to be regarded with more seriousness. The leading virtues in a married couple were listed as faithfulness, mutual respect and understanding. Sex and good housekeeping also appeared on the list, but much further down. Unsatisfactory sex was not considered a good reason for divorce, whereas sexual infidelity was. A happy sexual relationship was considered important by about 50 per cent of those questioned.

By and large, the British public showed themselves conservative in their attitudes: 76 per cent believed that women with small children should stay at home and look after them, and 19 per cent felt that women with teenagers should do the same.

An opinion poll survey carried out for the *The People* in October 1985 purported to reveal the 'intimate secrets' of 1000 married men and women. One 'intimate' secret revealed was that people now expect an awful lot from marriage. We are no longer content to co-exist with somebody towards whom we feel lukewarm or indifferent; we feel we have the right to be madly in love, and that marriage should make us happy, fulfilled and secure. If a marriage does not live up to these expectations, couples will not hesitate to head towards the divorce courts. No longer will people tolerate – as their forebears did – a miserable marriage, or one where there is no compatibility.

The newspaper spelled out, in order, the nine most important ingredients of a happy marriage, as revealed by its survey. These were give and take; treating each other as equals; liking each other as friends; staying in love; staying faithful; good sex; having individual interests; financial security; and children.

These all sound reasonable, but what do they really mean?

'*Give and take*' seems to be what does *not* happen in the average marriage, however much the partners hope it will. Whenever an old married couple celebrating a golden wedding is asked the secret of a successful marriage, the answer is always 'give and take'. To give and take really means to be tolerant, to have the best interests of the other person at heart. How many people do that? More often than not, individual wishes prevail and a power struggle develops, with one partner trying to dominate the other while the dominated partner struggles to assert individuality.

Very often it is the man who takes and the woman who gives. At least, that is how the wife usually sees it. The husband more often sees it the other way round. He sees himself (if the marriage follows the traditional pattern of breadwinning husband and dependent wife, as fewer and fewer do) as giving everything, providing everything, and getting precious little in return.

The main problem in modern marriage is that the majority of people are desperately hungry for love. They want constant assurances that they are loved and wanted and held in respect. When the husband comes home and finds his meal is not on the table, he becomes angry because this means he is not loved enough. When the wife discovers he has forgotten her birthday yet again, she is angry because this means he is not thinking of her. People demand respect and love from others when they have little for themselves. But you cannot demand respect. You cannot even demand give and take.

Genuine give and take in marriage can be hard to find. What often happens is that there is a trade-off: I will have sex with you tonight if you buy me that new dress tomorrow; I will have your boss to dinner if you take me to the ballet. These are crass examples, of course, but they serve to illustrate the principle. Give and take, in the average marriage, usually means bargaining positions and power struggles, in which both sides tend to end up feeling miserable and cheated. So much is expected of the other person – generally more than he or she is able to give, and we are deeply disappointed when our partners fail to come up to the mark. Yet why *should* somebody else be expected to fulfil our fantasies?

'*Treating each other as equals*', the second 'ingredient' of a successful marriage according to the survey, is fundamentally impossible in the context of marriage. Embedded in the marriage laws themselves is the concept that men and women are *not* the same and *not* equal. The only way in which a man and woman can stay equal is not to marry, but to remain single. Marriage, by its very nature, is an arrangement which renders the two parties unequal. It is only in the twentieth century that a married woman has even been considered a person at all. In the past, she was little more than one of her husband's goods and chattels. Her property, if she had any as a single woman, became his, while his remained his, on marriage. (Personal possessions such as clothes and jewellery did not constitute property.) We may imagine things have improved, but in reality little has changed.

As the law does not see married men and women as equals, so it is impossible for them to regard each other as equals. A woman is usually expected to join her husband wherever he goes, to support him emotionally, to believe that everything he does is right. Even today, a wife cannot be compelled to give evidence against her husband in court. Many wives will stand by their husbands even when they have been accused of cheating, consorting with prostitutes, lying, even murder. This happens because, in the majority of marriages, the woman becomes more dependent and attached than the man – and often truly imagines she cannot live without him.

If you want an equal relationship, do not get married: once married, you simply will not be allowed by society or by the law to remain equal.

'Liking each other as friends' was the third ingredient suggested by the survey.

Yes, this is really the ideal. But again, it is impossible in the average marriage. Why? Simply because you are forced to be so close, so emotionally involved, so financially entangled, that friendship becomes impossible. Many wives of famous men, when interviewed, will say, 'My husband is my best friend.' By that, they often mean that this man is their *only* friend: they have in fact forsaken everybody else and are often physically isolated, to the extent that friendship is almost impossible after marriage. Many married women simply do not go to the theatre, the pub, or any place of entertainment unless the spouse is there as well. They become actually incapable, in time, of doing anything on their own. And if their husbands work very long hours they find themselves virtual prisoners in their homes, passing whole days and evenings without seeing or speaking to anyone else.

'Staying in love' was the next requirement listed by the survey. The idea of being perpetually in love, in the romantic sense, is actually impossible for more than a very short space of time, as Mary Archer so rightly declared in her interview. If being 'in love' continues, it becomes an obsession, almost an illness. We like to promote the idea of being in love because we believe this emotion elevates us as human beings. It is a fine emotion to be able to love, but not to be in love. That is a selfish, high-arousal state of short duration, and it should be acknowledged as such.

'Staying faithful' was requirement no. 5. Most married people put a high value on sexual fidelity, because they would far rather their partner never so much as looked at another man or woman. The feeling comes from insecurity. Fidelity in marriage is now (and has always been) extremely rare. Though there are no reliable figures, newspaper surveys tend to reveal that at least 30 per cent of wives have affairs (of those who will admit to them) and the number is probably even higher for men. The problem is that it is absolutely impossible to feel both highly passionate and highly sexed and remain faithful to one person. Men and women who are sexy will almost certainly have affairs at some time in their marriage.

'Good sex' came next in the survey's conclusions, but although this is now seen as a vital ingredient of a happy marriage, it would not have been thus viewed in the past. Whenever people look to their marriage partners to fulfil their sexual fantasies, they are bound to be disappointed. Even the wildest, most ecstatic sex life dulls with repetition, as we all know, and the only real way to obtain 'good sex' (for those who see it as important) is to have a variety of partners – which does not quite square with the other requirements mentioned in the survey. In asking for fidelity, good sex and a good friendship, people ask for the moon. They are quite simply expecting far too much.

'Having individual interests', on the other hand, really is

important. Contrary to what people like to believe, most married people do not become more like one another as the years go by. For partners to try to pretend they have identical interests is only a recipe for disaster. Yet many have the idea that they must share everything: they go on holidays together even when one hates the place or type of holiday chosen, and one partner will try to bamboozle the other into pursuing the interests or activities that appeal to him or her. Maintaining individual interests is a far preferable idea, though very few couples seem to manage it.

'*Financial security*' was also mentioned on the shopping list of 'ingredients' for a happy marriage. Most of us would like financial security, but we are fools if we expect marriage to provide it. Girls have traditionally dreamed of marrying rich men. Those who did often discovered there was a high price to pay for access to the riches. The Bible tells us that it is harder for a rich man to enter the kingdom of heaven than for a camel to go through the eye of a needle. The reason for this saying, which is not very popular in an age when financial success is seen as the only sort worth having, is that material riches often make people believe they have more power and influence, and are more important, than is really the case. Rich husbands often treat their wives badly, as they see them as yet another possession, as something else they can buy. There is no greater inequality in marriage than financial inequality, and one's partner's possession of wealth does not make for any kind of security for the one who has nothing. The only financial security any individual can be sure of is that provided by himself or herself. Any other assumption is dangerous and can lead to rows and disappointments.

Is financial security attained when your spouse provides for you with insurance policies and pension schemes? Not necessarily: money can always be lost, as leading financiers have often found to their cost. At least the *People* readers had the sense to put financial security in marriage near the bottom of the list.

'*Children*', which appeared ninth and last in priority in the results of the survey, are a contentious subject. Readers were wise to put them at the bottom of their list. As we marry for 'happiness', so we have, or say we have, children for the same reason. But all the surveys show that couples without children are at least as happy as those with, and tend to stay together longer. Children do not and cannot bring happiness; neither can they cement a disintegrating marriage, although their presence might ensure that couples stay together longer than they might otherwise have done when things have gone wrong. Children are very often seen as part of the kit, something one 'goes in for' after marrying – and sometimes before or outside wedlock. As Princess Anne bluntly put it: 'Children are an occupational hazard of being a wife.' In the old days, people married mainly in order to have children, to continue the line, to have more hands to work the land, or to provide heirs or marriageable daughters. Now, those reasons for having children have largely gone, and most people do not know why they have them. We are told by infertile couples that they 'desperately' long for children, but we rarely ask them why. Children are supposed to crown a couple's happiness, but we can see all around us glaring evidence that this is rarely the effect they have.

Children can be a joy, it is true, but are they an ingredient of a happy marriage? I doubt it. It seems to me that children, particularly nowadays, cause more problems than they solve. Certainly they can never act as adhesive, to bring couples closer together, as some erroneously imagine.

Whether or not there are children in the picture, husbands and wives, people who are supposedly 'in love' and 'devoted' to each other, do some awful things to one another. The stories that follow are typical of our daily diet of newspaper reading. Feature pages carry a never-ending stream of articles about what makes a happy marriage, but the news pages bear witness every day to the true consequences of that togetherness.

In October 1985 we read in the papers the story of Nicholas Boyce, a highly educated 38-year-old, who cut up his wife and roasted bits of her so that she would look like the remains of a Sunday lunch. At his trial, Boyce described how he had endured months of misery before the final blazing row that made him mad with anger and drove him to murder.

Unholy Matrimony

Throughout their marriage, it was said, his wife Christabel had taunted him by saying that he was useless in bed, a rotten father and a 'lazy heap'. In his defence, Boyce claimed that he did two jobs, almost all of the family shopping and washing, and was forced to sleep on the kitchen floor. In the end, he became so enraged that he strangled his wife with a piece of electrical flex.

Christabel, it appears, had not wanted a divorce, even though the proposition was mentioned frequently. After killing her, Boyce tried to dispose of her body as a former wife-murderer, Dr Hawley Harvey Crippen, had tried to dispose of his wife's body – and with similar results. Both were found out.

There was a strange twist to the story. Christabel Boyce had been nanny to Lord Lucan's children – and Lord Lucan, it will be remembered, apparently tried to kill *his* wife, or perhaps hired a hit man to do it for him.

One might suppose that such stories are few and far between. They are in fact all too common. In 1987 Mrs Margaret Keating gave evidence in court against her former husband, who, she said, had tried to turn her into a human fireball by blowing her up. She suffered burns over 28 per cent of her body when her car exploded. The husband, Alistair Keating, aged 38, was also accused of inciting another man to arrange for his wife's lover to be beaten up. Mr Keating, the court heard, loved his wife and had tried hard to keep the marriage together. The couple had separated in August 1985, then attempted a reconciliation before separating for good.

Nor are vicars, supposedly advocates of marital monogamy and sexual fidelity (the principle of 'forsaking all others' mentioned in the marriage vows), exempt from straying themselves. By no means do they always practise what they preach. The Rev. David Osborn, a father of four, was accused of having an affair with one of his parishioners – and shocked his entire congregation. 'You don't expect such things of vicars,' said one of his parishioners.

A civil servant, allegedly of 'impeccable character,' strangled his wife at their dinner table after an argument over the mustard, a court heard. Thomas Corlett, 58, grabbed his Austrian-born wife Erika by the throat and shook her to the ground. After she

Marriage today

died, Corlett called an ambulance and told the police: 'It was her fault. I always placed my newspaper on one side of my plate, the mustard on the other. But she moved my paper and put the mustard in its place instead, saying, "That's where I want it and that's where I will put it."'

'She started shouting and kept on and on about the paper. She raised her hand and I thought she was going to hit me. I just grabbed her by the throat and we fell to the floor.' At the time of his wife's death, Corlett was an executive at the Department of Employment. His superior described him as quiet and conscientious, keeping himself to himself.

His late wife had suffered from asthma and, as a result of this, Corlett had had to help more with the household chores. At the time of her death Erika Corlett was also taking medication for anxiety. Corlett was jailed for three years, after being found guilty of manslaughter on grounds of diminished responsibility. In his defence, Corlett described how his wife increasingly irritated him with her annoying habits, such as leaving embroidery threads all over the floor and scattering face powder around. She also committed the terrible crime of going on holiday without him.

It is not only husbands who resort to desperate means to try to get rid of spouses that no longer please them. In April 1987 Chester Crown Court heard that Mrs Christine Buckley took out a £25,000 bank loan to hire an assassin to kill her husband, William Buckley, aged 50. The hired assassin shot Mr Buckley in the head at close range when he returned home from a prayer meeting. The trouble began, the court heard, when Mrs Buckley got tired of her husband as he increasingly chose to attend prayer meetings instead of social functions. Three years previously, Mr Buckley had joined the Salvation Army, renounced alcohol, and taken up the trombone. Mrs Buckley decided she would not put up with it and, in a pub one evening, asked a female friend if she had any of the weedkiller paraquat, which has so often featured in husband-and-wife murder stories.

The conversation was overheard by David Ashbrook, a used-car dealer, who said he would do the job if the price were right. A deal was struck and a sexual relationship developed between Mrs

Buckley and Ashbrook. Jailing the two for life, Mr Justice French said: 'This was a brutal and carefully planned murder. The plan was carried out in a remarkably cold-blooded way both before the killing and after it.'

Although murderous spouses often deny the existence of intent to kill, and that they did not know what they were doing at the time, it is very often the case that the murder, or murder attempt, has been carefully planned. The violence is almost always the result of several years of misery, at least on the part of the spouse who resorts to murder.

So strongly do the husbands and wives of today feel they own one another that they reckon they are entitled to seek any kind of revenge if one partner goes off with somebody else. In a dramatic court case, Dr Brenda Davies was accused by Mrs Helena Savvides of stealing and seducing her husband, Angelo. Mrs Savvides, a former Christian Dior model, complained that the doctor had wooed him away from her (Helena) while treating Angelo for a cocaine addiction. Dr Davies said in her own defence that she became emotionally involved only after she had finished treating Angelo – and that in any case the couple's marriage had been over, to all intents and purposes, for a considerable time.

Mr Savvides told the court that his marriage had effectively finished eight years earlier, and that he had told his wife many times that he wanted a separation. For years, he said, they had led separate lives. The upshot of this peculiar and murky case was that Dr Davies was cleared – but the idea that somebody could 'steal' a spouse remained. You can, of course, only steal something which belongs to somebody else. Our society seems to promote, in every way possible, the idea that marriage constitutes ownership of people.

Although men often turn violent when their marriages break down, such violence does not always take the form of wife-murder. In Seattle, Washington, Raymond Kirkman hired a bulldozer and reduced his marital home to rubble after he and his wife broke up.

It took Raymond just 15 minutes to bulldoze the house, which he did in response to his wife Sandy filing for divorce. Sandy,

Marriage today

aged 26, said: 'I told him I wanted to keep the house. I guess he didn't want me to have anything. We were all out of the house when he arrived, and in a quarter of an hour it was demolished.' Earlier, Ray had bought a demolition permit for the house.

In Victorian days there were many, many cases of husbands and wives trying to poison each other. At that time divorce was far more difficult to obtain, and for a desperate spouse poison may have seemed to be the only way out. But poisoning still goes on. In 1985 a husband sprinkled weedkiller over his wife's breakfast cereal after a row over money. Margaret Watkins, aged 52, had become enraged at her husband's spendthrift ways and ordered him to sell his expensive car and motorbike. John Watkins, a bus-driver (also aged 52), was a compulsive spender who owed thousands of pounds in hire-purchase money but would not sell anything to pay off his debts.

So, the court heard, he sprinkled his wife's All-Bran with sodium chlorate. When Margaret tasted her breakfast cereal, it was suspiciously salty and she contacted the police. Traces of the poison were found both in the cereal and in Mrs Watkins' body.

Poison has been the favourite husband-remover with wives down the ages – and so it remains, according to the evidence. Women tend to favour non-violent ways of murdering unwanted spouses. Recently a mother of five, Janet Barber, aged 48, was put on probation for three years after she poisoned her husband's raspberry crumble 'to shut him up for a few hours'.

The judge decided that she had been considerably provoked by her loud-mouthed husband, who went to sleep after Janet put twice the lethal amount of anti-depressant medication into his meal. He was later rushed to hospital, and Mrs Barber told police: 'I didn't mean to kill him. I put it in on impulse.' In fact her husband survived the incident.

In another case a driving instructor was jailed for life after murdering his wife and 13-year-old stepdaughter. The jury at Liverpool Crown Court heard that Robert Healey had struck his wife at least fifteen times with a rolling-pin and had throttled the girl.

After the murders, Healey had himself faked a suicide at

Prestatyn, North Wales, grew a beard and assumed a new identity after burying the bodies nearby. At the trial, Healey described the week-long rows that regularly occurred in this marriage – his second – and how he had tried to patch up the relationship by repeatedly sending his wife Greeba bunches of flowers.

Sometimes wives willingly help their husbands to commit suicide. In July 1987 a case came to court in which a woman's reaction to her husband's suicide threat was to pack a bag with whisky, lager and pills and take it into his office for him. When, later, he told her that he had been unable to go through with the suicide, her reaction was to say: 'I knew you had no guts.' In the event, when the couple came to divorce, Mrs Diana Kyte's award was reduced to £5,000 because of her attitude towards her husband's life.

In August 1987 a husband was jailed for four years for poisoning his wife with contaminated chocolate on Valentine's Day. Ian Walker, 36, took his revenge after the couple had had a blazing row, and gave his wife a Bounty bar which had been dipped in caustic soda.

His wife Rosemary, 32, took the chocolate bar when she left for a holiday with their two young sons; she bit into it soon after they reached their destination, began to vomit immediately and was taken to hospital with severe burns to her mouth and tongue.

During the case, heard at Exeter Crown Court, it was revealed that the chocolate bar contained enough poison to kill Mrs Walker. In his defence, Walker told the court that the whole episode was a joke, and that he had no idea it could cause so much harm.

He was jailed for four years for poisoning with attempt to injure.

Hell hath no fury like that of a man or woman scorned. Husbands and wives are all too likely to commit serious crimes when they discover that their partner has been 'cheating' on them – that is, has formed a close relationship with somebody outside the marriage.

When marriage partners are caught straying, there are two

Marriage today

common reactions. One is to try to get the erring spouse back, and the other is to try to get at least one of the offenders out of the way – either the adulterous partner, or the new lover.

Caroline Besley was one of those who tried to get her husband back. When she discovered that her husband, her former childhood sweetheart, was having an affair, she stole a total of £38,000 from the building society at which she worked and used the cash to wine and dine him and to shower him with gifts. In the event, all she got for her pains was a two-year jail sentence for fraud. The thefts, which were cleverly carried out in 200 bogus transactions, went on for nearly two years. Mr Greg Taylor, defending, said that the only way Mrs Besley felt she could keep her husband was to lavish money on him. 'But,' he added, 'it's a mystery where the money has gone.'

It is however more common for violence to occur after a husband or wife has been discovered to be having an affair. A jilted husband was put on probation at the Old Bailey in June 1987 after he stabbed his wife to death when she left him for a lover.

David Quiller, 36, was found not guilty of murdering his wife Yvonne, but guilty of manslaughter on the grounds of diminished responsibility. Yvonne had left him after ten years of marriage to set up house with their lodger. Quiller began to suffer from chronic depression and, on a visit to his wife's new home, stabbed her twelve times with a kitchen knife. The lodger, Robert Stephenson, was an old schoolfriend of Quiller.

A company director, Nigel Kraty, was also found guilty of manslaughter when he killed his wife's lover; he was jailed for 18 months. The jury at Reading Crown Court heard that he put up with his wife Janet's affair for ten months before he snapped, bought a shotgun and blasted his rival. Mr Justice Pain, summing up, said: 'The jury has decided that, in this dreadful moment, you were not in control of your mind.' Janet Kraty and the unfortunate lover, Michael Beeston, fell in love after she began having her hair done at his salon in Bracknell, Berkshire.

Sometimes it is the lover who wants to get the husband out of the way. John Walton was jailed for life for the murder of his lover

Unholy Matrimony

Marion's husband, Michael Joannou. Joannou, a wealthy publican, was found by his daughter Lorraine on the lawn of their home in Thames Ditton, Surrey. Marion, Joannou's wife, was jailed for eighteen months for trying to help her lover escape from justice.

During the case, the court heard that the couple's fifteen-year marriage had been extremely stormy, and was marred from the beginning by infidelity, beatings and other forms of unreasonable behaviour. In her defence, Mrs Joannou said that her husband beat her, wanted her to take part in wife-swapping, and regularly had affairs with other women.

When her husband's body was first discovered, Mrs Joannou put on a distraught wife act, appealing for help in finding her husband's killer, while Walton, who had been posted abroad for two months, went to Cyprus. (He was in the Life Guards, stationed near the Joannous' home.)

These few cases give an indication of what goes on, possibly more often than we realize, behind the scenes of marriages which may, on the surface, seem happy and successful – or at least all right. In none of these cases was there a trace of real love, respect, care or concern for the marital partner. These were people who had lived in hate and strife for several years and who were eventually driven to breaking point, when they committed a sometimes terrible crime.

Of all the crimes that are brought to court in any one year, a high proportion of them will be domestic. In fact, it is said that about 70 per cent of all serious crimes committed take place in the matrimonial home. Not all husbands and wives are driven to violence or murder, of course, but many are sorely tempted, and many experience moments when they feel that life would be easier and more pleasant if the spouse were permanently out of the way.

These feelings arise because we invest so much in marriage – in 'making it work'; naturally we are deeply disappointed, even enraged, when all our efforts seem to come to nothing, or are unappreciated. A husband may slave at his job for fifteen hours a day to give his wife 'everything' only to find that while he

Marriage today

has been out building up his business she has been carrying on with her hairdresser, the lodger, an old schoolfriend or a neighbour.

A woman may consider that she has 'devoted' the best years of her life to being a good and faithful wife, giving up her own career, cooking her husband nice meals and trying to be passionate in bed, only to discover that on his late nights 'at the office' he has been having an affair with his secretary or a high-powered career woman he has met. Such discoveries usually lead to highly emotional scenes – quarrels, recriminations, anger, jealousy, resentment and lasting hostility.

It appears that modern marriage brings out far more negative than positive emotions. What is usually seen as 'love' between two people who are married is often not love at all – it is a degraded, vice-ridden form of the emotion. Those who truly love somebody else will simply let them be free to develop their own personalities, to do as they wish – even if that includes being physically unfaithful.

People are horrified when they find evidence of a spouse's affairs; the discovery makes them afraid. All through the marriage, they have thought they owned the other person and controlled his or her life: the affair is evidence that they do not. We try to cling to other people when we have little self-respect and self-confidence. We vainly hope that the other person will give us what we lack – forgetting that the other person is, like ourselves, a fallible, weak human being who is probably unable to cope with such demands.

Those who are strong, and who value themselves, will be able to see the person they have chosen to live with as a friend, as somebody who is entitled to live a life of his or her own and with whom they can be civilized and respectful at all times. Very few modern marriages fall into this category. The 'commitment' we expect from a marriage partner is similar to a commitment to jail: it prevents our being free individuals. We are serving a sentence, supposedly for life.

Of course, not all marriages follow this pattern. But the majority will have elements of this negativity in them. We have come to feel it is right to be so bound up with another human being that every single thing he or she does, every twitch of the face, every fleeting expression, intimately affects us. Many wives live in constant fear of their husbands' anger, just as many husbands are terrified if their wives become depressed, or 'frigid', because these emotions mean that there is a cut-off, that communication lines are no longer open.

Modern marriage is in a parlous state, as any marriage guidance counsellor or divorce lawyer will confirm. It stifles individuality, encourages us to tell lies, to practise deceit, and to be manipulative, cunning and child-like, all because we live in fear that this (usually) rather ordinary and unremarkable individual whom we have married will do something that rocks the boat – be cross, not speak, throw things around, generally make life unpleasant, or go off with somebody else.

A moment's reflection will show that it is ridiculous that so many people should allow their lives to be ruined, even prematurely ended, as in the cases described earlier, just because they cannot see how to co-exist with somebody to whom they said, 'I do' a few years previously.

The discredited Indian guru Bhagwan Shree Rajneesh said that one reason why he never married was because 'all wives and husbands come to hate each other in time'; judging by the evidence available, this is largely true.

Marriage guidance counsellors, sex therapists, advice columnists and many others have pondered the matter of how to make marriage work better and with less acrimony and distrust between the partners. The newspapers, television and radio carry lengthy debates about what constitutes a happy, perfect marriage.

Usually, the only way we can envisage marriage working is if it 'goes back' to how we think it used to be, with breadwinning husband, dependent wife and total fidelity. It is commonly assumed by traditionalists that the main reasons why today's marriages are not working is because women these days want to be financially independent, have careers and maintain their individuality. If they were content to put their families first, goes the argument, all would be well. It is extremely unlikely that marriages of the past which did follow this pattern were happy – or even that women of previous centuries were as loving and giving as they were made out to be. Even a cursory reading of novels by famous Victorian writers will give an impression of marriage that differs substantially from the fantasy we fondly carry in our heads.

As I write, the press has been giving considerable attention to marriages being arranged between British men and Filipino girls. Nothing could more vividly illustrate the mismatch of hopes and expectations than that which occurs in these marriages. Each Filipino girl who eagerly answers an advertisement placed by a European male seeking a traditional type of wife imagines she will be transported into a world of wealth and luxury where, as Lesley Garner wrote in the *Daily Telegraph*, a 'charming, unchauvinist liberated Western male' awaits her. Instead, she is likely to find an 'unregenerate macho Brit expecting a submissive, unliberated Oriental woman'. The probability of disappointment is obviously high. Whereas in such cases the woman may expect a more equal partnership than would be possible with one of her own countrymen, the husband-to-be is often in search of little more than a housekeeper who provides sexual services. 'Illusion plays a great part in most marriages,' wrote Lesley Garner. 'These transcultural marriages involve more illusion than most.'

She also commented: 'An equal adult relationship does not seem to be the object of the quest. Nobody going into a marriage bureau for a girl from a poverty-stricken country can be looking for an intellectual companion or soul-mate. At best, they [the men] seem to be yearning after a nice, old-fashioned, ignorant girl.'

Men and women, fed by romantic fantasies and illusions, both yearn for marriage to be some kind of safe haven, where they will be protected from the harsh outside world. People yearn for this in marriage as they used to pray for it in their religion.

Christian hymns abound with injunctions to the Lord to keep us safe from all the perils and dangers of the world. 'Safe in the arms of Jesus' has been translated in our modern times to being safe in the arms of a loving spouse.

Unholy Matrimony

It is a current cliché to say that we have substituted love in marriage for the love that used to be reserved for God. Modern marriage is in a parlous state because we want and expect so much of each other, yet never stop to consider whether our marital partner is actually capable of providing what we want. There is no way to make marriages work better while we bring to them false hopes and expectations.

Any attempt to bind people closer together, by law or by custom, is bound to fail. People become violent and hateful towards each other when they are deeply disappointed. We buy a dream – and all too often end up with a nightmare.

In her almost painfully honest book *Deceived with Kindness*, Angelica Garnett, daughter of Vanessa Bell and Duncan Grant, describes her marriage to 'Bunny' Garnett, 26 years her senior:

> The story of our marriage could be summed up as the struggle on his side to maintain the unlooked-for realization of a private dream, about which, in spite of an almost wilful blindness, he must have had deep misgivings: and on mine the slow emancipation from a nightmare, which was none the less painful because I thought of it as almost entirely my own fault. . . . Had I not married him, he would have been a perfect friend, one in whom I could have safely confided and who would always have given me good advice.

'At bottom,' she continues, 'my love for him was simply a delusion – a dream which I had not the strength to sacrifice... I saw myself being swept along by a dangerous current, but was unable to lift a finger to prevent it . . . I knew inwardly that I was doing the wrong thing.'

Angelica concludes that what she had found was not life, but a backwater. Sadly her experience is not an isolated one. When I look at the marriages of most of my friends and acquaintances, I can see all too clearly that they are living a nightmare, one which, frequently, they have the courage neither to admit nor to escape from; they are living with the consequences of a ghastly mistake.

Marriage, at least in its present form, fails all of us. How much better relationships between the sexes would be if we truly could be friends, as Angelica Garnett realized she could have been with Bunny, and did not feel this overpowering need to tie ourselves together in Gordian knots.

3

Marriage through the ages

There is a widely held belief that the institution we call marriage has always existed in pretty much the same form: that two people meet, fall in love, get married and try to live happily ever after, raising their family and supporting themselves with work of one kind or another.

In fact, though male and female sexual unions have been with us ever since time began, the institution of marriage has, as we shall see, weathered some extremely far-reaching changes over the centuries. Virtually the only constant feature of marriage is that a man and a woman come together for reproductive purposes.

But the way in which such unions have been arranged has been subject to more permutations and changes than any other man-made (in this case literally made by males) institution.

In one society monogamy is the norm while in others polygamy is considered the 'natural' way for men and women to relate to each other. In a very few societies, such as in the mysterious Buddhist country of Ladakh, polyandry – in which the woman has more than one husband – is practised. In Ladakh, the birth-rate has stayed the same for hundreds of years and polyandry is no doubt practised because the arid and largely inaccessible land simply cannot support more than a very small population.

In some societies, husbands and wives have been expected, indeed required, to love each other, to enjoy sexual relations with each other and to seek comfort in each other's company. Other societies, such as that of Ancient Greece, have considered the only true and noble love to be that between men, and women to be useful only in so far as they can procreate and look after the household.

At certain times, marriages have been able to take place only to the accompaniment of elaborate rituals and complicated financial exchanges. At others, the 'love is blind' idea has held sway, the only important factor being that the partners love each other. In some ages (in Britain, for example, before 1563 and the Council of Trent, when couples made a simple agreement to cohabit and had no ceremony, either secular or ecclesiastical) and in some present-day societies (many parts of Africa, for example), marriages have taken or still take place simply through two people deciding to live together: their verbal agreement was and is considered binding.

Then again, divorce has been a simple matter in some societies and almost impossible in others. It is still the case in Islamic societies that men can divorce their wives merely by saying, 'I divorce you'. Divorce is almost as easy for the women, too, except that they have to wait three months so that it can be ascertained that they are not carrying their ex-husband's child.

Although the one absolute in marriage is that a man and a woman come together for the purposes of sex and procreation, there is one other: in almost every society, marriage benefits the man far more than the woman. Feminists are fond of calling marriage *per se* a patriarchal institution and there is little evidence to refute this. In virtually every marital arrangement the man is seen as superior. As Chapter 5 will demonstrate at greater length, every kind of marriage appears to have been ordained by men, for men and on behalf of men.

The idea of what constitutes a 'proper' marriage has changed radically down the ages, but its assumption of male superiority has never basically altered.

There is no general agreement on what marriage means, except that it involves some kind of subjection of the woman to the man who, for some reason hard to fathom, is universally seen as more elevated, more worthy, cleverer and in every way more competent than his wife. The concept of sexual union is also intrinsic to the idea of marriage, and those in which sex does not take place can be annulled or dissolved. Sex has, from the very earliest times, been seen as an inescapable and necessary ingredient of marriage. In traditional and early societies, sex was regarded not as a mutual pleasure or 'fulfilment' of the relationship, but as a means of continuing the species. The idea of sex for pleasure has now largely supplanted that of sex for reproduction, and many couples now decide that their union shall be childless. In the past, it was seen as a great curse and misfortune not to be 'blessed' with children. Nowadays, children are regarded very much as a mixed blessing; they are sometimes seen more as consumer items rather than additions to the family workforce or heirs to a lineage.

The popular idea of marriage in the West is that a man and woman meet, marry and set up home together. In the East it is very different: there the woman does not just marry the man, she marries into his family and goes to live in her husband's house. It is not always realized that until recently this was the norm in continental Europe too. Only in Britain and its colonies have married couples tended to live by themselves after marriage. The notion that married couples should set up home on their own has been common in British society for hundreds of years, but until modern times it was somewhat alien to the rest of the world.

In the rest of Europe, until the twentieth century and the industrialization of society, which caused people to move about in pursuit of work, a wife went to live with her husband's family. She would take a dowry, whereas he would inherit land. The idea of primogeniture, whereby only the eldest son can inherit property and estates, is considered normal in Great Britain, but highly peculiar and unfair to many people in other countries. However, in virtually no country in the world do daughters inherit equally with sons. When daughters are given a portion of an estate, this usually comes in the form of money rather than land.

In past ages, before any welfare or social security service became established, the family took responsibility for everything, including care of the young and elderly, production of food and clothes, animal husbandry and crop-growing. The family was in fact the basic economic unit. While this was the case, there was not all that much room for love and romance in marriage. A man would want, above all, to marry a woman who could produce fine sons and bring a sizeable dowry – or, in the lower classes, pull her

Unholy Matrimony

weight with the weaving, spinning and dairy work. A woman would want a strong and healthy man who could farm crops, who would not be lazy or get drunk, and who would treat her well and respect her.

In the often harsh economic climates of the past, when hospitals, schools and state benefits were unknown, there was little time for sentiment in marriage. It was above all a practical arrangement, conducted on business-like and pragmatic lines. In the Middle Ages the only place where romantic love found expression was in courtly circles between people who were not, and who would never be, married to each other. Marriage was in those days considered too serious a matter for the uncertainties of love. Besides, earthly love might have interfered with heavenly love, which was in theory the universal aspiration. For the courtly lovers, earthly love was considered but a step on the way to divine love. This has its apotheosis in Dante's *Divine Comedy*, in which the heroine, Beatrice, leads her poet lover up to heaven.

At a later date, the secular love poems of John Donne give way eventually to 'a hymn to God the Father' and other works in which the poet agonizes over his relationship with God.

The pages that follow briefly relate how the idea of marriage changed radically in England from the Middle Ages to the present, and then go on to compare the situation in Europe and Japan.

The British idea of marriage is important not just to Britons but to much of the rest of the world, as it was carried to North and South America, Australia, New Zealand and, later, parts of Africa. Even though Americans have now established their own marriage laws, their starting point in the seventeenth century was the Protestant, largely British, concept of a good Christian marriage.

The American scholar Lawrence Stone has written a monograph entitled *The Family, Sex and Marriage in England, 1500-1800* which has become the classic reference work on the subject. Stone, like so many historians, appears to feel that we have made considerable progress in our attitudes towards marriage during the three centuries in question, and seems to see it as a good thing

Marriage through the ages

that what he calls the patriarchal marriage gradually gave way to the companionate marriage, in which the relationship between partners is more equal. But have we really made that much progress? On the whole, married people seem to be as unhappy with each other today as ever they were. And have the days of the patriarchal marriage ended? In many ways, marriages seem to be as patriarchal as ever. Anybody who disputes this has only to look at *Burke's* or *Debrett's Peerage* to see just how very much more important men are considered to be than women. And of course, whatever happens at the top of society filters down to the ordinary untitled and non-landed gentry.

In that men are no longer allowed by law to beat their wives (using a stick no thicker than their thumbs – hence the expression 'rule of thumb'), and that women are now allowed to earn a living and to own property, we have perhaps made some progress. But we appear to have made precious little in our ability to make a success of living together harmoniously. The National Marriage Guidance Council, now renamed 'Relate', is unlikely to find itself out of business in the foreseeable future.

The so-called 'companionate' marriages mean that we expect a lot of each other, whereas in the past, when marriages were more or less arranged, expectations were few and husbands and wives were not thrown upon each other's resources to anything like the extent they are today. Could it be that men and women are not actually *meant* to live in symbiotic union?

Lawrence Stone claims in his book that in the past British marriages were cold, distant and patriarchal, while sex was by and large considered a sinful necessity, to be endured, not enjoyed, by each party. In the sixteenth century, he declares, both men and women would have been very surprised to hear that an ideal marriage was one in which the partners had fallen in love with each other. The poets, especially the so-called 'silver' ones of that period, spoke endlessly of love, of course – but the object of the affections was never a wife. Marvell may have written, wooingly, 'Come live with me and be my love', but in reality romantic love was considered a kind of mental illness, something young men had to get out of their systems.

Unholy Matrimony

In the days when married people lived in extended households, which could include aunts, uncles, grandparents, servants and possibly livestock, relations between married people were often not very intimate at all. There was simply too much hard work to do and hardly any privacy. It was assumed in those days that sexual desire, where it was unfortunate enough to exist, could be satisfied by just about any member of the opposite sex. Being in love, or even feeling physical attraction, was certainly not a prerequisite. According to Stone, the typical sixteenth-century family was an 'open-ended, low-keyed, unemotional, authoritarian institution which served certain essential political, economic, sexual, procreative and nurturant purposes'.

Going even further back, we find that the pre-Christian Anglo-Saxon societies were very casual indeed about marriage. It was merely a private arrangement between two families who might consider it prudent to join forces for economic or dynastic purposes. Property exchange and responsibility for children (future inheritors) were the primary consideration and those whose families possessed property and land were automatically considered a better catch than those whose parents were landless and poor.

For several centuries after Christianity came to Britain, this casual approach to marriage continued. The church ceremony which, until recently, was considered essential to a 'proper' marriage, was then regarded as an expensive and unnecessary luxury. It was certainly not required to render the marriage legally valid.

By the thirteenth century, however, the Church had begun to consolidate its authority and to consider it had every right to regulate personal and sexual relationships. It was during that century that the idea of a monogamous, indissoluble union started to take hold. Previously, divorces were virtually as easy and casual as marriage itself. Britain had, after all, been under Roman occupation for four centuries, and the Romans were strong advocates of divorce.

In the late Middle Ages, Stone tells us, marriage was not in any way an intimate kind of union, but an arrangement whereby the married partners thenceforward came into daily and close contact with all the relatives of the spouse. Romantic love, lust and affection were all regarded as extremely ephemeral and untrustworthy reasons for entering into marriage. Marriage meant, above all, a transfer of money or land. Relations between the spouses were remote and not necessarily very friendly.

There was no single recognized form of marriage in those days, and in fact marriage could take many forms right up until 1753, when Lord Hardwicke's famous marriage laws (Lord Hardwicke's Act) were passed in Parliament. Until this date, a couple could be considered legally married if they had made oral promises to one another, known as 'spousals', or if their parents had drawn up a contract regarding financial arrangements. The only prerequisite for a valid marriage was sexual consummation.

For the rich, ceremonies would usually accompany the property exchanges, but for the poor a betrothal was considered binding without the sanction of the Church. Church marriages were very much an optional extra until 1562, when the Reformation introduced several new ideas about marriage. One of these was that for the first time marriage became a holy sacrament, heralding the new age of Protestantism and anti-Catholicism. Archbishop Cranmer, who was largely responsible for the marriage service as we know it today, widened the concept of marriage to include mutual comfort and help and spiritual intimacy. In the past couples had been bound to each other by duty and service to the family. Now they were expected – indeed obliged – to love one another, and the premise that women were subordinate to their husbands became enshrined forever, almost as if it were the natural order: women who feared God would naturally want to subject themselves to their husbands, as if that were what God had ordained, in his infinite wisdom, for them – a holy duty.

The marriage service which has become most famous is, of course, that contained in the *Book of Common Prayer* of the Church of England.

'Dearly beloved,' it begins, 'we are gathered together in the sight of God, and in the face of this congregation, to join together

Unholy Matrimony

this man and this woman in holy matrimony.' The first part of the service goes on to say that marriage between men and women symbolizes the union between Christ and the Church. Does this mean, then, that marriages between non-Christians are not ordained by God? The service continues by saying that Christ 'adorned and beautified' the marriage in Cana (where he turned water into wine); but Christ himself never married – he remained celibate for the whole of his life. The marriage service states quite categorically that the institution is not ordained to 'satisfy men's lusts' – and yet many people today consider that this is exactly what marriage is for. What it *is* for, we are told, is 'the procreation of children', so that they can be brought up in the fear and nurture of the Lord. The text of the service also states quite clearly that marriage is secondary to celibacy, and is for those who 'have not the gift of continency': its existence enables their sexual appetites to be contained within a sanctioned institution. Nowadays, most people do not accept that belief: marriage, or at least togetherness, is seen as a higher form of existence than continency, or autonomy.

Thirdly, the service states that marriage is ordained for mutual help and comfort. Although this was considered the least important reason for marriage when the text was written, being placed third, it now comes first in most people's opinion.

In the original marriage service the vows made by men and by women are different. Whereas the man promises only to 'love her, comfort her, honour and keep her in sickness and in health', the woman has to promise to 'obey him, serve him, love, honour and keep him in sickness and in health'. When the service was first devised there was no real notion of equality. Inequality was in fact enshrined within it. This is emphasized by the fact that the woman has to be 'given' by a man to be married to her husband, which further strengthens the concept that the woman is a piece of property which is changing hands.

After the father or 'friend' has given the woman, she has to repeat again that she will obey and cherish this man. The instructions are that a ring shall be given by the man to the woman, not that rings are exchanged. The ring, a potent symbol of bondage, is to be worn by the woman only. Nowadays men often do wear rings, but this is nowhere near so common as it is for the woman to wear one. Many men refuse to wear a wedding ring as they think it makes them look like wimps – chained to their wives and possibly henpecked.

The vows end with the man saying 'With my body I thee worship and with all my worldly goods I thee endow.' In fact, the man is not in law bound to endow his wife with his worldly goods, although until recently the reverse was the case. When the man and woman make their vows, they have to repeat that they have decided to live together 'according to God's holy ordinance' – but *none* of this is in the Bible. After the vows have been exchanged the minister ends by saying, 'Those whom God hath joined together, let no man put asunder.' But of course, it is not God who joined them, but the Church and the law. Also, the marriage service is legally binding only if performed under the auspices of the Church of England. In all other places of worship – Catholic, Jewish, non-conformist – the local registrar has to be present.

In the original full service, following the exchange of vows, there are some lines purporting to come from St Peter, referring to the wife as 'the weaker vessel' and including the commandment: 'Ye wives be in subjection to your own husbands'. The service calls on holy writ here, alleging that Sarah was in subjection to Abraham and called him 'Lord'. (The fact that Sarah was not a Christian does not appear to matter.)

The last paragraph of the marriage service is virtually incomprehensible and I have never heard it used at a wedding. Even so, the idea that women are in subjection to men runs as a mighty theme throughout the whole service, without justification. If women are to be in subjection to men, this would indicate that the men are, by dint of their very sex, in some way superior to women. Yet no examples of this superiority are given in the marriage service.

The marriage service dumps all the hard work on the woman's side. *She* has to adapt herself to her husband, not he to her.

Even if I were a Christian, I could not see how the marriage service, composed in the reign of Queen Elizabeth I, came to be considered the word of God. No god who possessed the qualities normally ascribed to the supreme deity would be so sexist. There is after all no trace of sexism in Jesus' teachings, which form the basis of Christianity. But the marriage service is patriarchal, sexist, unfair, unrealistic, too demanding – a total confidence trick. Most people have got so used to hearing the words that they do not ever think about their meaning, or realize quite how pernicious they are. If the marriage service *were* the word of God directly revealed, we could perhaps pay more attention to it. But it is not.

Nor does it have any power. No couple married in church can claim to have a more 'perfect love' for each other than others married by a simple civil ceremony. The kind of 'love' encouraged by the marriage service is in any case not real love, since it depends totally upon female submissiveness. Yet the service is at the same time very clever, because it sanctions male ego and aggressiveness while giving female subjection, passivity and dependence a kind of holy aura. The 'holy' woman is one who is quiet, meek, loves her husband (whether or not he is loveable) and does not draw attention to herself in any way at all. The marriage service effectively wipes her out.

Because this Elizabethan marriage service is still in use (though it now includes some modern adaptations) it continues to colour our idea of marriage, and every time it is read out it reinforces the notion of male dominance and female subjection. The only wonder is that, over the centuries, so many women have gone along with it without complaining (and still do).

When this marriage service was composed it was not legally binding and was not to become law for another century and a half. But it set the tone once and for all.

Marriages from then on became idealized as founts of earthly paradise and partners were henceforth seen as one flesh – one entity in law. The husband acquired control of all his wife's property and finances and was responsible for all her debts.

Throughout the sixteenth century the status of women was in severe decline. While Catholicism was still the main religion there was at least some feminine influence – that of the Virgin Mary.

There had also been an alternative occupation to marriage for women: becoming a nun. The nuns of the Middle Ages were the great careerwomen of their time. Now this was all swept away. Most women were denied any kind of education, and the intellectual gap between men and women increasingly widened. The Protestant preachers of the time advocated total subordination of women, whose only functions in life were housekeeping and childbearing.

However, this did not mean that married women did nothing. In the lower classes they worked as hard as their men, though their economic contribution did not confer any status or power: women worked because they were bound by love and duty to their men and would do everything asked of them.

During this time arranged marriages were extremely common between royalty and the aristocracy. Thus Mary Queen of Scots was betrothed to Francis, heir to the French King Henry II, at the age of four, and was married to him at fifteen. She became Queen of France at sixteen and a widow a year later, when her young husband died of a brain abscess.

In her book *The Gospel According to Woman*, Karen Armstrong tells us that during the seventeenth century marriage obtained a completely new profile. It became almost a vocation in itself to marry and produce a family. Before this, when Catholicism was the official religion, marriage was held to be an infinitely lower condition than celibacy and monkhood. (Jesus never married and nor did many of his early followers, although he blessed the marriage at Cana by his attendance.) Until the Reformation the religious life was a valid alternative to the married state. Now, there was none. After the Reformation, women disappeared into the anonymity of marriage and were never seen or heard of again. No wonder Millamant in Congreve's comedy *The Way of the World* (1700) is reluctant to 'dwindle into a wife'. The lives and personalities, talents and productivity of women were completely absorbed by their husbands – a state which for the majority of women has not really changed all that much in our own time.

The idea of female independence became anathema, and all

women were supposed to be 'tidied up' into monogamous marriages. Spinsters were considered 'spare' women.

Thus, through Protestantism, the status of marriage acquired an extensive upgrading. Since then, it has never been knocked from its pedestal.

The doctrine of 'holy' matrimony meant, in effect, that the husband had total authority over his wife, and that the woman should be ready and willing to subject herself completely to him. At the same time, the concept of the family started to change in Britain from an extended to a nuclear one, in which the unit would consist of only the husband, wife and children of a single generation.

During the eighteenth century, however, states Lawrence Stone, another change occurred in the perception of marriage. The concept of duty gave way to that of romantic love. The pursuit of pleasure and self-fulfilment was no longer considered wrong. Repression and authoritarianism decreased and marital sex was no longer seen as important only for the purposes of procreation. Sexual intercourse, Stone tells us, came to be seen as a pleasure in itself. At the same time, there were major moves to contain sexual lust and sensuality within marriage, so that partners would not be tempted to stray outside the relationship for sexual satisfaction.

Gradually, marriage was becoming a far more complicated institution. It was still, first and foremost, an economic and sociopolitical consolidation; but it also embodied personal affection, physical attraction and, lastly, romantic love: a love which would blind the partners to each other's personal faults, lack of money and any other drawbacks.

The truly romantic marriage is aptly demonstrated in the life of the poet Percy Bysshe Shelley, who at the age of eighteen eloped with Harriet Westbrook, then later left her for Mary Godwin, daughter of the pioneer feminist Mary Wollstonecraft. Although of aristocratic origin, Shelley had no money or prospects when he married. He and Harriet soon started to reproduce. In the event, the romantic ideals turned sour very quickly. Harriet committed suicide, all but one of Shelley's and Mary's children died, and

Shelley himself died in a boating accident at the age of 30. The life of the poet Byron was similarly punctuated by 'romantic' attachments which tended to end in grief and death.

Before the romantic age was ushered in, it was popularly believed that physical desire and romantic love were 'violent mental disturbances which would inevitably be of short duration', as Stone puts it. And in truth, only a tiny minority of men and women ever married as a result of strong romantic passion. However, the growth of romantic literature in the late eighteenth and nineteenth centuries very much affected people's notions of what a proper marriage should be, separating once and for all the reality and the fantasy.

As more people learned to read and write and the mass media developed everybody started to imbibe romantic ideas of marriage. Women were the great readers of romantic fiction, as they still are. And the more avidly they read, the more likely they were to mistake male lust for romantic passion of the sort they read about in books. Mary Wollstonecraft, who might herself be considered to have made two romantic attachments, to Gilbert Imlay and William Godwin, regarded romantic love as a purely artificial emotion, invented by novelists and adopted by men as a cover for their sexual desire. Her view was that women should be content to love passionately just once in their lives, and then let the passion subside into friendship.

Certainly her daughter Mary took this advice. She fell violently in love with Shelley when she was sixteen, ran away with him to France, had a number of children in quick succession, wrote *Frankenstein* at the age of eighteen and then, after her husband's death, when she was only 24, simply never fell in love, or entertained the thought of marrying, again. Once was enough.

Lawrence Stone's view is that romantic love is not so much inbuilt as a cultural expectation. When marriage was above all a practical arrangement, very few people ever fell in love – or rather, they never fell in love with the person they intended to marry. After the romantic era, people expected to fall in love. They looked for it and, through looking, found it.

The eighteenth and nineteenth centuries consolidated the

perception of falling in love as something that was noble and pure, and no longer a form of mental illness. Earthly love no longer led to heavenly love, but was an end in itself, a goal worth pursuing.

With the growth of these romantic ideas, financial and property arrangements in marriage assumed less importance. A couple who loved each other would not want their union to be sullied by sordid financial arrangements. In Britain, by 1770, young people were largely allowed to choose their own partners – a freedom which did not obtain at this time in other parts of Europe, where parental wishes were still paramount. The Duc de Rochefoucauld, commenting on this in 1784, observed that in England:

> Husbands and wives are always together and share the same society. It is the rarest thing to meet the one without the other. The very richest people do not keep more than four to six carriage horses, since they pay all their visits together. It would be very ridiculous to do otherwise in England than it would be to go everywhere with your wife in Paris.

The British, he added, 'always give the appearance of perfect harmony and the wife in particular has an air of contentment which always gives me pleasure'.

The wives' apparent contentment would seem to suggest that they were trying to make a virtue out of a necessity. Women had very little option at that time but to marry and, in marrying, to subjugate themselves entirely to their men. In law they had no rights whatever after marriage. Moreover, divorce was virtually impossible and formal separations difficult to arrange.

Separations commonly happen, says Stone, where there are emotional expectations which have not been fulfilled. 'When expectations are low, frustrations will be low,' he writes.

If in the eighteenth century some lip-service was paid to the idea that husbands and wives should enjoy a more equal kind of relationship, this was suppressed by the Victorians, who largely denied that women could have sexual feelings and considered sexual desire generally to be something that should be stifled. Harsh physical punishments for children became the norm again, as they had been in the days of the Puritans, and wives were expected to bow to the absolute authority of their husbands.

The twentieth century has seen further changes in society's perceptions of marriage. We now believe, or claim to believe, that marriage should be a loving union between two equals, although the law does not support this idea. We expect a lot of marriage – emotionally, sexually and financially – but if the relationship does not appear to be working, it is pretty easy to obtain a divorce and start all over again.

Lawrence Stone comments:

Aspirations for sexual and emotional fulfilment through marriage have mushroomed; pre-marital sexual experimentation has become increasingly respectable, thanks partly to a dramatic improvement in contraceptive technology which has at last more or less successfully isolated sexual pleasure from procreation.

But the twentieth-century ideal of marriage has not produced more happiness and harmony than the more rigid unions of the past. Stone cites several factors which he believes, account for the low success rate of modern marriages: 'the isolation of the nuclear pair from external ties and friendships; the withdrawal from neighbours, friends and peer-group associates in the street and pub, the village shop or the church, and the physical and psychological detachment from relatives, including parents. The only thing that holds a pair together is what they can get out of each other in the way of emotional and sexual satisfaction.'

As has been increasingly apparent during this century, there is a limit to what one person *can* get out of another human being.

The stories about the Prince and Princess of Wales illustrate how degraded our notions of modern marriage have become. When the couple were first engaged, the press rhapsodized over their 'wonderful love', and they were endlessly pictured holding hands by mountain streams, staring out to the horizon from their honeymoon yacht or otherwise epitomizing togetherness. Lady Diana, the young, beautiful virgin, was seen as having the ability to breathe new life into the fast-ageing Prince Charles, enabling him to hang on to his disappearing youth. After the 'fairy-tale' wedding, Diana produced two sons in rapid succession – the 'heir and a spare' – and became the epitome of radiant young motherhood as well as one of the most beautiful and elegant women in the world. Her unerring dress sense, model's physique and natural beauty made her the most sought-after cover girl for magazines the world over.

There has been speculation, however, that after seven or eight years of marriage all is not well; the couple no longer want to be together all the time, it seems. Is the fantasy of their marriage falling apart? Or have they simply done what all married couples do in time – grown up, got used to each other, and developed an urge to go, at least to some extent, their separate ways?

They do, after all, have different interests. Charles, who is thoughtful and introverted by nature, enjoys sport and is concerned with many topical issues, including modern architecture and inner city renewal; he is also inclined to mysticism. Diana enjoys the ballet, restaurants, choosing clothes, pop music – all the activities of a typical young woman of her age.

Harold Brooks-Baker of *Debrett's Peerage* was quoted in *The Sunday Times* (24 October 1987) as saying that Charles and Diana's marriage was virtually arranged. It is well-known that Diana had to fit certain criteria, notably that of having no 'past', to be considered suitable for the role of wife to the future sovereign. An element of 'arrangement' would in any case have been in keeping with royal tradition. Until the nineteenth century, all royal marriages were arranged, and there was no question at all of 'love' playing an important part in the selection of a partner. Politics were the prime motivation, especially if the royal families of different countries were involved. It is also accepted that adulteries were traditionally tolerated in royal marriages and that only since George V's reign has marital fidelity been expected of either partner. So for Charles and Diana to have been in love is a comparatively novel phenomenon.

But we won't allow them – or anyone else – to pass to the second stage of love. We insist that married people should either be tied together in a romantic love-knot or wrenched apart in an acrimonious divorce. In our late twentieth-century concept of marriage there is little room for manoeuvre between the two extremes.

The mainly British ideal of romantic love has been enthusiastically adopted by the rest of the world. But although it has been current in the UK and in America for more than 200 years, it is comparatively recent for other countries. The concept of the nuclear family is also new to much of continental Europe, as well as to the Middle East and Far East.

Michael Mitteraner and Reinhard Sieder, two German academics, claim in their book *The European Family* that the idea of a family consisting only of a man, a woman and their child or children simply did not exist in Germany before the end of the eighteenth century.

Peter Laslett writes in his introduction to this book that in England every marriage necessitated the setting-up of a new household rather than a further addition to the established family home. Strangely enough, one can see the idea of the extended family in action in the television soap operas *Dallas* and *Dynasty*, in which everybody appears to live pretty much under the same roof. Southfork, in *Dallas*, is a multi-generation, multi-family home where all the members of the family sit down to meals together, served by faithful uniformed retainers. This is probably how (give or take a little wheeling and dealing) the average upper-class European family would have lived, although it was never a reality in either Britain or America. It seems likely that the extended-family household in television soap operas exists merely to meet the demands of the storyline, in which warring factions must continually interract. This would be difficult if they all lived miles away from each other in separate establishments.

In Austria and Central Europe the servants, too, would be considered part of the household, and were very often related to the head of the household. The 'family retainer' would be somebody actually related by blood – again, an idea which is unfamiliar in Britain and North America.

Mitteraner and Sieder observe that the family is commonly seen as a static structure incapable of great change, and is popularly conceived as a human constant, a natural and normal way to live. But, they add: 'It is impossible to consider it [the family] in any way a 'natural unit of human communal life, remaining the same over time.' The Latin word for family means essentially the house, rather than its various occupants. The concept of the family changed radically when the home and place of work became separated after the industrial revolution. Industrialization changed the family structure from many to few members. The later the industrial revolution hit, the longer the multi-generational family remained the basic unit of society. In Russia, for instance, the generational family lasted far longer than in many European countries, while in China and India it is still the norm.

Today's typical nuclear family of man, woman and two children may remain unchanged for many years, but in extended households, and particularly in peasant communities, there was little stability: hardly a year passed without some major upheaval. People were always getting married, and hence going to live in another extended-family household, or becoming servants or assistants in other people's houses. Children of one household often went to live as short-term servants in somebody else's house, even when they were of equal social standing.

In the days of the extended, rapidly changing household, relationships tended to be formal and distant. It was not wise to form close bonds. Husbands and wives were separated, often for years on end, when men went to fight in wars. On the other hand, bereavement did not have the same shattering effect on families as it does today because there was always somebody else to carry on the work. The death of a marriage partner did not spell loneliness and isolation for the one who was left – there were always plenty of other people around.

Children, too, departed and died with great rapidity. There was in the typical traditional European family little closeness between husband and wife, marriages often being arranged for convenience. It was also common for there to be a great disparity in age between partners – and the wife was by no means always younger. Servants and older relatives continued to exert a significant influence within the household. The authors of *European Marriage* comment tellingly that psychoanalysis grew up only after the extended family had largely been replaced by the nuclear one in Europe. 'Increased intimacy', they observe, 'possibly often leads to psychological disturbance.'

Today's family, they say, has become far more susceptible to crisis. In families where personal relationships are less intense, with a 'less closed and a less intimate atmosphere, such disturbances [are] less likely'.

What happened in Europe, the authors explain, is that the authority of the head of the household was gradually eroded by the state, as the state took over many functions which were formally confined within the family. The religious function of the family was the first to lapse. The authors say that the old idea of the large family was founded on ancestor worship, and the characteristic family cult was the house cult, with household gods. The establishment of organized religion took this function away from individual families.

Blood revenge by adult males – so much a feature of Norse and Icelandic sagas – and family feuds of the Romeo-and-Juliet type also disappeared. Romeo, it will be remembered, could not marry Juliet because their respective families, the Capulets and the Montagues, were sworn enemies. In Anglo-Saxon times and the Middle Ages such situations were common, particularly in Europe, and parallels can be seen even today in areas where different religious factions are at loggerheads.

The protective functions of the family were also eroded. In the old days, hospitality would be extended to a stranger. This still happens, of course, in some countries – the poorer the country, the more likely it is. Large families also used to offer sanctuary, on condition that the stranger submitted to the authority of the head of the household.

The economic functions of the family have largely disappeared, too, in industrialized societies. Households used to be individual economic units; now they are simply places to live, eat and sleep while the work of earning a living is carried on elsewhere.

The family's responsibility for education has ceased to exist, though this development occurred far later in Europe than it did in Britain.

The reproductive functions of the family have also altered

considerably. Formerly, children were needed to work and be economically active as soon as possible. Now, children are a drain on their parents' financial resources: they are an expense rather than providers of labour.

Lastly, the cultural functions of the family have undergone great change. Families once had to defend themselves against human enemies in addition to cold and hunger. Nowadays, leisure is seen as essential, we have gardens which serve no economic purpose, we take holidays for no particular reason and pursue economically unnecessary activities such as golf, sailing, mountaineering and skiing. We keep animals as pets rather than to make sure we have enough food to last the winter. The family has therefore become a unit of consumption rather than a self-contained contributor to the economy.

In the typical European family of the past, a rigid patriarchalism ensured that the male head of the household was given due authority. Sons were preferred to daughters as they could carry on the line and also fight if necessary to defend the family's territory. Now, say the authors, with the decline of the old-style family, patriarchalism is also in steep decline. Many feminists would, of course, hotly dispute this.

But Mitteraner and Sieder consider that the old concept of extended families continues even today, when that pattern of co-existence has long since vanished. They write:

Under conditions of advanced industrialization, we can find ourselves saddled with a procreative pattern that was justified in the peasant household but is no longer wholly appropriate. Ideas about the upbringing of boys and girls still hold sway that have their roots in the long-lost division of labour between husband and wife within the family. Claims to inheritance and property that were legitimate in a social world that has long disappeared still retain their value. Such a cultural lag is often to be noted in the history of the family because of its inherent conservatism.

Another major change that has occurred is that, increasingly, we are belonging to cultural groups that have nothing to do with the family. The idea of the peer group has grown rapidly during the twentieth century. Adolescents now commonly dislike being with their families, and prefer to move in circles comprised of people of their own age groups. Men have office colleagues and friendships while many married women, the last group to be emancipated from the home (though the process is not yet complete), now have their own careers and are part of networks that tend to consist of other women. Old people, nowadays, tend to gather together in retirement towns or in sheltered housing, or in old people's homes. The different generations and different sexes no longer have to interact together to keep the family unit viable. Indeed, the modern idea is that young people should leave the parental nest as soon as possible, to set up a separate bachelor or marital home.

Individuals within the family are now freed from rigid parental control and family influence is no longer paramount. The young now claim their status and their amusement outside the parental home and no longer respect their elders. But where families continue to operate as the basic unit of production, freedom of the young to live their own lives simply does not exist.

In India, for instance, it is still common for sons to continue the family business, and to bring wives into the family household rather than establishing their own. For traditional families, there is little thought of doing anything else, although in major cities such as Delhi and Bombay families are becoming fragmented and no longer multi-generational.

As the large family unit declines all over the world, there is a tendency for married people to become far more dependent upon each other. Love and marriage are no longer separated, as they were in societies where arranged marriages were the norm. In Europe in the eighteenth and nineteenth centuries it was common for husbands to have mistresses and wives to have lovers – often quite openly. Marriage was for reproduction and continuation of the dynasty, while love was sought elsewhere.

The romantics regarded love as the main justification for marriage. Gradually, this idea that love must be an ingredient of marriage has become almost statutory, and a 'loveless' marriage is seen as one that should be allowed to end as quickly as possible.

Unholy Matrimony

In Japan, until very recently, marriages were extremely rigid. Before the Second World War, when the concept of marriage changed forever in Japan, the continuation of the 'house', which really meant the dynastic line, was paramount, and both custom and obligation played their part in the conduct of events.

Joy Hendry's book *Marriage in Changing Japan* charts for Western readers how the idea of marriage gradually underwent a dramatic change as Japan itself altered from a rural to a highly industrialized society. In the old days people married to carry on the line or to cement alliances. They were usually arranged by a go-between, and the question of the partners' choice was not a relevant factor. Moreover, the idea that sexual gratification could be sought within marriage would have seemed very strange. 'Love,' writes Joy Hendry, 'was considered an emotion on the same level as the mating of animals and marriages based on this notion were generally considered to lead to great unhappiness for all concerned.'

For many centuries in Japan sex outside marriage was condoned, even expected, for men, and concubinage and prostitution were accepted practices. This changed when Japan became subject to Western, specifically Christian, influences, which condemned this as wrong.

In old Japan men took concubines as a status symbol, in much the same way that they might buy a Porsche or the latest hi-tech gadget nowadays. The offspring of such unions were legally recognized and were serious contenders as successors to the existing head of the household. Concubines were legally abolished in 1882.

Of course, as in other countries, the double standard applied in Japan. Although concubines were the order of the day for men, women were not expected to take lovers. Indeed, until 1908, a husband who discovered his wife had been unchaste could kill both her and her lover without fear of punishment. Women were taught that their prime duty was obedience to men, and in poor families it was considered an act of supreme self-sacrifice by a girl if she sold herself into prostitution to help her family out financially.

Under the old laws a wife who failed to fit in, or to satisfy her husband or the rest of the household, could be returned to her parents. She was, for some time, considered to be 'on appro'. Divorces were easy, but in many households the wife's status was too low for her to be a serious nuisance. If the alliance between families was seen to be sufficiently important, an unsatisfactory wife would be kept on regardless, in order to avoid breaking the alliance and, possibly, inviting a bloody revenge.

Marriages were often not recognized until a baby had been born and the wife had thereby proved her usefulness as a reproductive machine.

That was old-style Japan. Nowadays the dynastic approach has largely vanished and marriages increasingly follow the Western model of choice. Costly receptions and white wedding dresses have also become extremely popular. Western ideas of romantic love spread gradually throughout Japan: as late as 1930 one writer could say that it was 'moral weakness to fall in love, effeminate and unmanly'. The Samurai tradition held that marriages of choice were barbaric and completely against correct conduct.

After 1947, when Japan gained a new constitution, the traditional foundations of the family system were abolished and many of the old ideas were swept away. Both male and female children now had an equal right to inheritance, replacing the old idea that all property should go to the eldest son. A modern couple could choose either surname, and parental consent was no longer necessary for those over twenty wishing to marry.

The Japanese family unit has now become nuclear, and most couples have no more than three children. Even that, says Joy Hendry, is often seen as one too many. Many women now have outside jobs and proper careers, although sons are still commonly preferred to daughters – perhaps because of the outdated idea of kinship: taking on responsibility for the welfare of the whole extended family.

But some things in Japan have not changed. It is still common for men and women to seek their entertainment separately, as it is in the Middle East and India. And couples still expect far less of each other than in Europe and America. It is considered enough if couples get on reasonably well together and are sexually compatible enough to produce children. They do not have to be all in all to each other. Joy Hendry compares the average relationship of husbands and wives to that of a civil servant and a politician. She notes, too, that girls are encouraged to prepare themselves for marriage rather than develop individual talents which will enable them to be independent and self-sufficient.

As in most modern families all over the world, Hendry says, a household without women is far more at a loss than one without men. It is still regarded as highly peculiar in Japan for men and women not to be married. In the area where Hendry carried out her field studies, she found only three adults over 30 in a whole Japanese village who were unmarried, and all these were single for health reasons. 'Young people of both sexes,' she writes, 'regard marriage as inevitable.' The old-style go-between, or marriage broker, has not disappeared and still plays an important part in arranging marriages.

Even though Japan has now adopted many Western customs in relation to marriage, Hendry observes, there is still no word in their language to correspond exactly to our 'love'. The term *ren'ai,* which denotes sexual attraction, comes nearest. Yet only a small proportion of marriages in modern Japan are based on *ren'ai.*

The main premise that Japan had adopted from Western ideas of marriage is that of individual happiness and fulfilment. In the old days duty and obligation to the family, and to the code of honour, prevailed, and there was little notion of pursuing happiness or fulfilment for oneself.

In both modern and traditional Japan almost all events fall into one of two categories, joyful or sad, and are celebrated accordingly. Marriage, however, is considered to have both joyful and sad connotations. On the one hand, the union of two people, and possibly two households, is considered cause for celebration; on the other, the bride has to leave her own home and go into that of her husband's family, live in a strange household and share her bed with a man she may hardly know. The husband's family will also have to make adjustments to accommodate this newcomer within the household. The bride is considered 'reborn' when she marries, and henceforth wears different kinds of clothes to indicate her new status. In the past, wives were also expected to shave their eyebrows and blacken their teeth. This tradition no longer survives.

In Japan, as in all other countries and traditions, past and present, far more of an adjustment is needed on the part of the woman than on that of the man when a marriage takes place. The wife assumes the identity of her husband in a way that could never happen in reverse.

The institution of marriage carries a heavy historical burden. It seems, from this brief historical survey, that it was ordained in order that communities could consolidate and strengthen their position. All the historical arguments in favour of marriage now seem to have disappeared yet, strangely, we still cling to it.

Today, large numbers of people have no religious belief, yet still we adhere to the basic Christian idea of marriage – which has to a significant degree permeated the rest of the world. Even civil weddings held in registry offices have a veneer of religiosity. It is now becoming common for those undertaking their second, or even third, marriages to have them 'blessed' in church by a priest, which would have been unthinkable even as recently as the 1950s.

It seems we are left with the empty shell of an institution which has no real purpose in the modern world. People can function and exist just as well without marriage as with it. The only reason it has survived for as long as it has seems to be that the inspiration of romantic fantasy has prolonged an otherwise superannuated institution.

At one time it was virtually a necessity for men and women to marry, and thenceforth to raise families in an established household which could defend itself against human enemies and physical disasters. There was safety and strength in numbers. Now that the state has taken over most of the former functions of the family and we no longer need older sons to inherit and to defend territory, there seems little justification for continuing marriage as an institution.

4

The tyranny of togetherness

In past ages, as we have seen, relations between husbands and wives tended to be formal and distant, even to the extent that partners would address each other as 'Mr' and 'Mrs'. In Jane Austen's *Pride and Prejudice* Mrs Bennet always calls her husband by his surname, as do Mr and Mrs Hardcastle in Goldsmith's *She Stoops to Conquer*. In employing such forms of address, literature was merely reflecting the custom of the time.

Formal modes of address, of course, indicated a formality of approach which extended throughout every aspect of life, and which was the norm in almost all Western countries until relatively recently. It was the proud boast of many Victorian wives that their husbands had never seen them naked. Now, we affect to think this shocking, an indication of repressive and rigid behaviour: we believe that nothing should be hidden between husband and wife. In place of distance and reserve, we have a form of cosy coupledom previously unknown. Husbands and wives, at least in the West, are expected to share every aspect of their lives, to have no secrets from each other – financial, emotional, physical or professional. It seems natural and normal today to discuss everything with one's spouse, to hammer out problems, to communicate all hopes, fears and desires on every level, in the pursuit of true intimacy. It is an intimacy which simply never existed in the past.

Current received wisdom tells us that such intimacy between men and women who are married to each other, or are living together in a long-term relationship, is unequivocally a good thing. Nowadays even formerly private activities such as taking baths and giving birth have to be shared. Those of us who are married are allowed to keep hardly any experience to ourselves, even that of an affair with somebody else. A few years ago the idea of 'open' marriages, in which husbands and wives could have extra-marital affairs without guilt, shame, lies, secrecy or subterfuge, was seriously mooted and a few people actively adopted it. Although the practice never became widespread, it reflected a general feeling that secrecy between people who lived together and shared a bed was a bad thing, while total openness was good. Openness in fact reflected closeness.

The kind of closeness which is now expected between married couples is unique to this century, and would have been considered highly odd – possibly, like falling in love, a sign of mental disturbance – in past ages. We believe that if a husband and wife are together all the time, never taking separate holidays, never being apart if they can help it, they must truly be in love and must truly care about each other.

Conversely, those who are content to spend a great deal of time away from each other are considered to have a most peculiar and probably rather unhealthy relationship. If a famous couple, such as the Prince and Princess of Wales, spends a few weeks apart, the newspapers start asking if their marriage is on the rocks. Anything less than supreme delight in and constant demand for the other's presence is to indicate that all is not well.

In *The Sunday Telegraph* Mary Kenny observed:

Historically and anthropologically, it is the notion that husbands and wives do everything together which is unusual. The His-and-Hers marriage, in which the couple is as inseparable as a pair of twins – ever synchronized in thought, word and deed – is a very recent American invention of dubious value.

In most societies and at most times husbands and wives have lived very separate lives. All through the Islamic world men and women, even when married to one another, are normally apart. As Germaine Greer has pointed out in her book on fertility, more women throughout the globe sleep with their children than with their husbands.

There are whole tribes in which men and women speak a different language, or a different version of the same language. In rural Ireland, until very recently, men and women ritually sat on different sides of the church, and this reflected the norms of life: a man's place was not with his wife but with the menfolk.

Those people who prefer to be individuals, to do their own thing, to wander off alone, nowadays tend to be those who do not marry. One of the most famous examples of a man living the bachelor life to the full is the former British prime minister Edward Heath, who has been categorized as a relentless hobbyist for his love of activities such as sailing and music. It is commonly assumed that anyone who pursues such interests with dedication must be using them as a substitute for a close relationship with another human being. A close, stable heterosexual relationship of a permanent nature is today seen as the norm, while anything else is considered a deviation.

In the old days explorers were content to leave their wives and families alone while they tramped across uncharted wastes. Now, cosy coupledom has to obtain even on Antarctic expeditions. Sir Ranulph Fiennes, one of the best-known explorers of recent times, almost always goes on his expeditions with his wife Virginia. Another explorer, Robin Hanbury-Tenison, was accompanied by his second wife on a trip to China. Dervla Murphy, a female explorer who has never married, told me once that travelling in pairs was a mistake, because people you meet put a bracket round you and ignore you, she said, whereas if you are alone you see more, hear more and make more friends than you would if you had a close travelling companion. Real exploring, one imagines, has to be done alone, which runs contrary to current thinking about married couples.

There is hardly any area left in life where you can be alone or just with members of your own sex. A large proportion of former boys' schools have become co-educational and the old-style single-sex grammar school is virtually a thing of the past. Just about all Oxbridge colleges are now co-ed, and virtually all professions, with the exception of the Anglican and Catholic churches, are now equally open to both men and women.

Good or bad, this tendency underlines the fact that whereas

society used to allow the sexes some breathing space from each other, nowadays they are allowed none at all. Today's couples are allowed no freedom, no respite from one another. It was hoped at one time that co-education and freer communication between the sexes would lead to a greater understanding, better relationships, and a lessening of hostilities, but this has not happened. Nobody could argue that present relationships between the sexes within marriage are better than at any other time in the past. This century has seen an unprecedented number of marriage break-ups, usually to the accompaniment of enormous acrimony, and the trend shows no sign of abating.

One reason for the high rate of failed marriages is surely the degree of closeness that our society encourages – a closeness not even the most understanding and tolerant relationship could stand. Moreover, it goes against human nature to chain oneself to just one other person for the whole of one's life. Most of us have harboured, at some time in our lives, the fantasy of finding just one special person with whom we could spend the rest of our lives, without our ever wanting to look at or be with anybody else. In fact, we all need the opportunity to be apart, to be able to converse with members of our own sex and have confidant(e)s of our own gender. Yet society expects us to need no comforter or adviser other than our own marital partner. We are not even supposed to want the company of other people once we have decided to form a permanent partnership. Once we marry or set up home together we are assumed to be one inseparable couple rather than two individuals who happen to be living together for practical and reproductive reasons.

Whenever women in the news want to give the impression that they have a wonderful marriage, they will say that their husband is, quite simply, their best friend. Modern, or 'new', men are encouraged to think the same, though they do not tend to express this friendship ideal quite so readily. There is perhaps a lingering suspicion in men's minds that men and women are not really buddies, and that the most enjoyable friendships for them are with other chaps, with whom they can talk about cars, cricket and football – all the topics which most women find terminally boring.

The tyranny of togetherness

Centuries ago the Greek playwright Aristophanes wrote that humankind could not bear very much reality; perhaps the truth of the matter is that human beings cannot bear very much closeness, particularly if they are of different sexes. Those who embrace it as an ideal soon find that the closeness becomes cloying and that the once-joyful intimacy turns to resentment, hostility and a continual feeling of malaise. About 30 million prescriptions are issued every year in the UK alone for tranquillizers of some kind – sedatives, sleeping pills, anxiety reducers. Almost all of these are provided for married people who, on the surface, seem to have nothing wrong with them. Doctors often write such prescriptions when they cannot diagnose anything specific, and yet it is clear that the patient is suffering. Many of the people who turn to tranquillizers because they are unhappy are those who have built up in their minds an ideal of what marriage should be but found that the reality is very different. Yet instead of advising partners to take time off from each other, to allow each other space and freedom, doctors prescribe pills and the conventional advice from advice columnists and marriage therapists is for couples to try doing things which will bring them even closer together. Nobody seems to want to acknowledge the truth of those old sayings 'Familiarity breeds contempt' and 'Absence makes the heart grow fonder'.

So deadening is the weight of this expectation of togetherness that all boys and girls over the age of eighteen who do not have at least a semi-permanent partner are likely to be considered – and consider themselves – somewhat lacking. What is it about unattached individuals, people wonder, that makes them unattractive or unappealing to the opposite sex? Today, young people are thought to be normal if they are able to attract large numbers of the opposite sex. Equally, they are considered peculiar if they simply succeed in attracting members of their own sex (despite 'gay liberation') and are considered to be 'unable to form proper relationships' if they show no inclination to make exclusive alliances with either sex.

Yet all this pressure to court and date, and the recent upsurge in 'singles' bars and 'singles' holidays – which are so called only because their function is to turn people into doubles as quickly as possible – bear witness to the fact that nobody is allowed to face the world as a single person any more. The minute a marriage or other long-term relationship ends, people are encouraged to join a computer dating service, a marriage bureau or a divorced-and-separated club where they will, it is hoped, find somebody to team up with before long. The lengthy columns of 'lonely hearts' advertisements in many newspapers and magazines attest to the fact that society considers it highly abnormal for any of its members to be unattached. Whatever your character or interests, however peculiar you may be, the message is that somewhere out there another human being is waiting to team up with you in an intimate, exclusive way.

Whenever people consider they are moving apart, they instantly assume something is wrong; some seek outside help, often from people who are incompetent to give it. Advice to go on second honeymoons, to take up a hobby together, to try new tricks in bed, rarely works, because when a partner feels generally miserable within a relationship it may well be because, perhaps unconsciously, he or she is trying to uncouple.

The American sociologist Diane Vaughan has written a remarkable book called *Uncoupling* in which she says that wherever there is a feeling of malaise and discontent in a partnership the process of uncoupling has already begun. 'Uncoupling' does not necessarily denote a chain of events that will end in divorce; moreover, Vaughan wisely observes that many couples who divorce are still by no means uncoupled, but remain much attached to each other, at least emotionally. Some relationships, writes Vaughan, never really come apart, even after the death of one partner. Yet almost always, she claims, the intensity of the relationship is one-sided. It is almost impossible for two disparate human beings to want the same level of closeness. Virtually the only time this happens is with identical twins, who are in a biological sense almost two parts of the same person.

According to Vaughan, almost all relationships begin to uncouple at some stage. The trouble is that the partners are unlikely to admit this, even unconsciously. So the process continues under cover, as it were, until a point is reached when the discontent cannot be hidden any longer and one partner asks the other for a divorce or begins to lead as separate a life as possible. When this stage is reached, discord and acrimony are likely to occur and the long, painful process of joint uncoupling must begin.

In our society we assume that all uncoupling must be bad, a sign that something is wrong. But Diane Vaughan has noticed that uncoupling of one kind or another is a near-universal phenomenon. Individuals feel uncomfortable in a too-close relationship which is supposed to be so fulfilling and elevating – yet, because of the pressures, both direct and indirect, that are put on everybody to be part of a happy couple, they will often not acknowledge it.

If we did not feel we had to be so intimately involved in the first place, the process of uncoupling would not be so traumatic and life-shattering as it tends to be today.

We have come to feel that close coupledom is the natural way for adult humans to relate to one another, and in the West this is certainly the ideal. Yet it is not so, even nowadays, in the East, where boys and girls are virtually never allowed to be alone in each other's company until marriage – and then spend as little time together as can be arranged. In India, for example, it is quite common to see two men walking down the street hand in hand. Yet you never see a man and a woman holding hands in public, even after they are married. Such public displays of affection and attachment would be considered highly unseemly and undignified. Of course, clandestine affairs do take place: men and women who are neither married nor likely to be do fall in love, and pre-marital virginity is probably far less universal than might be hoped. Even so, as a society India does not encourage the intimate coupling of men and women to the exclusion of all others. The average Indian household encompasses lots of other women and lots of other men, so that a married couple is hardly ever thrown on its own exclusive resources. (This might suggest that India therefore has a very low divorce rate: it has, but this stems from the fact that Indian women are conditioned from birth to tolerate whatever a man does and to accept that they will always be under a man's control – first their father's, later their husband's.)

For all our supposed intimacy, sharing and caring, it appears that relationships between husbands and wives are at least as bad as they have ever been, and may well be worse. Many of us who spend years of our lives 'working' at a relationship are shattered when we realize that the effort has been to no avail. Many women, particularly, in the West, suddenly recognize in their thirties or forties that they have, as they see it, wasted long years of their lives in the pursuit of 'togetherness' within a long-term relationship when they would have done better to develop their own talents and careers.

But the triumph of hope over experience can be seen in the remarriage figures. Almost everybody who divorces eventually remarries, and thus starts the whole process over again – usually to face a similar disillusionment sooner or later. With second marriages, the disillusionment often happens much sooner. The trend is for second marriages to break up even faster than first ones – usually because the remarrying men and women have not given themselves time to sort out what they really want. They rush to marry again because they cannot imagine life on their own. Most of us are too frightened even to contemplate the idea. Yet many divorced people of both sexes have said that once they got used to it living alone was bliss.

Nowadays, we are expected to be able, and even to want, to share everything. Gone are the days when men and women had their own separate spheres of operation, with never the twain meeting. It is common now for husbands and wives to set up in business together, and many of these businesses are extremely successful. Laura Ashley and Body Shop are just two (very high-profile) companies which have owned their success in large part to the input of complementary male and female skills. Winners of the Veuve-Clicquot Businesswoman of the Year Award are often women who have set up their multi-million pound business together with their husbands, or long-term male sexual partners. Increasingly, doctors marry doctors, solicitors marry solicitors and social workers marry social workers, continuing a professional as well as a personal partnership after marriage. Often these partnerships do work: it makes sense, after all, to pair up with somebody with whom you have something in common. If two people living together have common interests, then they are less likely to find each other irritating than if they discover after a few years that they have nothing to talk about to each other at all and have, in the meantime, let all previous friendships wane.

But although these partnerships work for some people, they should not be taken as a blueprint for partnership success. Although artists commonly marry artists, and actors other actors, the divorce figures are frighteningly high in these creative circles. The danger is that because they work for some people, people imagine that these professional/marital partnerships should be able to work for everybody.

We are all different, and some of us are psychologically unsuited to forming an exclusive pair-bond (as Desmond Morris describes it). Some of us find such exclusivity stifling and a hindrance to establishing our own individuality. The biggest danger for all of us as individuals is that we become so submerged in the partnership, in coupledom, that we are unable to function on our own any more. We become like parasites, twisting ourselves round each other so closely that if one dies, the other will too – at least inside. The situation is far from healthy, yet it is encouraged nowadays at every turn.

Take childbirth, for instance. For centuries, this was an intensely private, all-female affair from which men were rigorously excluded. When the time for the birth drew close, the mother-to-be would summon the (female) midwife and would be attended by other women. After the child was safely born, the father would be allowed to see him or her, but he would be kept firmly out of the way until the processes of birth and its immediate aftermath had been completed. Few women are now allowed to give birth in this manner. Husbands or lovers are encouraged by hospitals and by those promoting home births to be present, often while video cameras record the event for posterity. Male partners are encouraged to massage the woman in labour, to administer to her needs and to remain with her throughout the entire process, even watching the placenta come out. Some hospitals now have 'family rooms' furnished with double beds, so that the new father can be there permanently, even sleeping in the same bed as the mother shortly after the birth.

Twenty years ago the presence of the husband at the birth was considered modern and daring; now it has become the norm. The French obstetrician Michel Odent, who believes in natural, drug-free birth, has challenged this notion, as he believes the presence of the husband goes against primitive female instincts. His views may be somewhat suspect, however, as most doctors, particularly obstetricians, like to be in sole charge of a birth, and if they are male may not take kindly to the presence of another man who might challenge their authority. Be that as it may, Odent believes that women's natural preference would be to give birth in a dark corner by themselves, in much the same way that cats do, greeting the world only when it is all over and they can look clean, tidy and presentable.

Even in childbirth, a woman is never allowed to be alone. Twenty years ago most men would have thought that to watch a woman give birth was distasteful in the extreme. Now they commonly say that it has been the most moving experience of their lives, which just goes to show how infinitely adaptable humans are, even emotionally. A growing number of men now write sentimentally in the press about the wonder of childbirth, and how things somehow never seemed the same again after they had witnessed the birth of their own child. Most say that the experience has brought them much closer to their partners, and that they feel they truly shared in the experience.

After the birth, modern fathers continue to play an active part. Parenting now has to be 'shared'. Men are now seen pushing prams (a sight that was rare even during the 'fifties when I was a child), shopping, cooking, cleaning the house and even being full-time househusbands.

Sharing the workload of parenthood and running a house makes a great deal of sense, since the age of domestic servants is long past and few of us can seek help from relatives living nearby.

The trouble is that this type of sharing is not simply regarded as a practical answer to living in the modern world: it has to be part of a highly-charged emotional togetherness. This new desire for closeness is, like so many other aspects of life, a currently convenient social construct. As the previous chapter has shown, the ways in which men and women relate to each other has weathered infinite permutations over the years. The new togetherness is just another permutation, no more 'natural' than any of the others, and ultimately it will destroy both partners, as the mistletoe does its host tree.

Because of this expected exclusive closeness, men and women nowadays are expected to put a great deal of time and energy into pleasing the partner – sexually, emotionally, practically and financially. We are expected not merely to remember anniversaries and birthdays, but to mark them with presents of more than merely sentimental value: cars, golf-club subscriptions and expensive jewellery. The latter, particularly rings, constitutes symbolic bondage. When women flash expensive rings given to them by their husbands or boyfriends they expect to arouse envy, but they are in fact advertising their pride in being possessed. I see the wearing of rings as pretty much the same as a bull having a ring through its nose, which enables the owner to do exactly what it likes with it. A ring given by a spouse is a sign of ownership.

The tyranny of coupledom exhibits itself in many everyday situations. First of all there is the invitation syndrome, which visibly reflects how we regard married or cohabiting couples as an indissoluble unit rather than as two separate individuals. When dinner-party invitations are sent out, husbands and wives are automatically invited together. If a person of either sex is invited to an opening night, a cocktail party, or a conference in a professional capacity, the invitation will usually read 'and guest'. In fact, Dr Miriam Stoppard – very much her own person – once complained that the words 'and guest' appeared so often on invitations sent to her husband, the playwright Tom Stoppard, that when people asked her name she said, 'And Guest'. Surely it is humiliating to be invited to a function simply because you are living with the person whose presence is actually desired. You know you are not attending in your own right, but as a makeweight, an individual in whom nobody is interested. And yet it is assumed that where one goes, the other must follow.

Such doubling up means that at any gathering there are usually twice as many people present as there should be. Normally, nobody thinks to question it. But what purpose does the presence of this other person there serve? Nowadays, once married, or known to be part of a cohabiting couple, we are treated as an indivisible unit forever.

There are many other ways in which the tyranny of coupledom asserts itself in the modern world. When politicians or heads of state go on trips abroad, it is common for their spouses to accompany them. Thus we often see Denis Thatcher walking behind his wife, looking somewhat awkward. Nancy Reagan and Raisa Gorbachev are usually by their husbands' sides. When Anwar Sadat was president of Egypt, his attractive wife Jehan often accompanied him on his trips. When party political conferences are held in Britain each autumn, politicians' spouses are always there by their partners' sides. During the 1987 general election in Britain, the wives of the three opposition party leaders were never far from their husbands. Mrs David Owen and Mrs David Steel – Deborah and Judy respectively – even went on television together to tell the nation how their husbands were coping with the election campaign, while Glenys Kinnock was constantly seen with her husband Neil as he campaigned. One wonders how these intelligent women, with careers of their own, could possibly justify what they were doing 'supporting' their husbands, especially when their presence or absence cannot in any respect affect the outcome of the election, the summit, the peace talks, or whatever. Anwar Sadat possessed in Jehan just about the most beautiful and charismatic wife a man could have, but it did not stop him being assassinated by Muslim extremists. Wives commonly feel they should support their husbands through thick and thin, but there is no gain of any kind in their so doing, either for them or for their husbands. Men also support politician wives, although rarely with the same intensity. But the conventional wisdom is that if you have a spouse, he or she should be there with you on every possible occasion. When we watch election results being read out on television, the wife or husband of the candidate is almost always close to the politician up for election, loyally wearing a large rosette. It is expected that the spouse of a politician should hold identical views and will be content to echo what the great man – or woman – says. Why do spouses have to waste their time thus, by attending on their higher-profile partners? In so doing they are curtailing their own individual development and imprisoning their own personalities in the partnership, to the detriment of both.

In politics, above all other fields of endeavour, coupledom is part of the kit. In America, some professional wives have even given up their own careers to help their husbands with their campaigns. This does not please Germaine Greer, who wrote bitterly against such behaviour in an essay in the book *Women: A World Report*, published to mark the end of the United Nations' Decade for Women. *A propos* of the situation in Cuba in 1984, she writes:

> People did not sell themselves as they do in consumer society. Life was not soap opera, but real. There was no competition or character assassination, as people jockeyed for limelight. They spoke not to persuade or bamboozle, but to explain. They had not our prurient interest in domestic or sexual affairs. No one was quite sure how many children Fidel [Castro] might have, or, for that matter, Vilma [Castro's sister-in-law, and a prominent female activist]. Public functionaries were assessed on their performance of their public duty, and did not have to drag their bed partners around with them, miming domestic bliss.

Some people were horrified when they read this comment in Greer's essay, but it has to be admitted that she is in this instance, as in so many, right. When 'bed partners' are dragged around by a political husband or wife, that bed partner is condemned to live a half-life, never quite knowing who he or she is. Denis Thatcher has managed to avoid this, perhaps simply because he is a man: a male spouse's identity is never eclipsed in this way, somehow. Prince Philip is another example: always very much an individual, and never merely the husband of the British Queen.

Unholy Matrimony

People like Jehan Sadat, Nancy Reagan and Raisa Gorbachev can never really know who they are or what their role is supposed to be. Owing to their total identification with their husbands they are forced to mouth sentiments they probably do not feel and undertake tasks which they would not otherwise choose. When their husbands die or lose office, these political wives commonly fade into the background and are never heard of again (Mrs Bandaranaike of Ceylon and Corazon Aquino of the Philippines are two famous exceptions). Theirs is only a secondhand limelight. As the American feminist Gloria Steinem once said, Americans call Nancy Reagan their First Lady, but nobody in Britain ever thinks of Denis Thatcher as their First Man.

These women behave like this because they think they ought to, and firmly believe they are doing what is right. But because they live such very public lives, they are in danger of setting an example which the rest of us should never begin to follow.

A spouse, we commonly believe, is somebody whose critical judgement over his or her partner is forever suspended. Even when (male) ministers are caught embezzling funds or having affairs, their wives are seen smiling wanly as they stand by them. Girlfriends of convicted criminals often say how 'gentle' and 'generous' their man was when he wasn't busy mugging or slaughtering other people. The feeling that one has to suspend one's own beliefs and analytical powers is uppermost in coupledom. Once married to a man or woman for better or worse, we hold to that quite literally.

Even women who have been married to truly despicable men will say publicly, 'But he was always a good husband' (whatever that might mean). They say this because, after marriage, they see themselves as one entity rather than two: the couple. The net result is that the wife of the well-known person can never truly be herself: hers is a life cut away – sacrificed – and for no good purpose.

We have come to assume in our society that men and women must move around in pairs. Coupledom has even got to the stage where lesbian and gay politicians are accompanied by their same-sex partners on campaigns. It seems to have become impossible to stand alone. Germaine Greer was castigated for her comments on Cuba by those who said it was just sour grapes because she had no partner. The implication, not in this instance valid, was that she could not attract one. Indeed, virtually anybody can attract a partner. Why otherwise would men like Hitler, Stalin, Rudolf Hess, Himmler, Idi Amin, Peter Sutcliffe (the 'Yorkshire Ripper') have been able to marry and, in many cases, father children? Most women would recoil in horror at the idea of an intimate relationship with any of these monsters – and yet, quite ordinary, pleasant woman did form such liaisons. Similarly, virtually every woman who wants to can find herself a husband. In *Macbeth*, Lady Macduff remarks, *à propos* of husbands, that she could buy herself one at any market. Nothing has changed: the difficulty in our society today lies not in the ability to *find* a partner, but being strong enough to do without one.

The tyranny of coupledom obtains in many spheres of life other than that of politics. In the armed forces wives are commonly expected to follow their husbands from base to base and from country to country in a way that cannot in any way benefit them (the wives). It is the same in, for example, the diplomatic service, many multi-national companies, academic circles and the judiciary. But why *should* women be expected to uproot themselves and move to different countries, where they have no real role and serve no real purpose, just because their husbands do certain types of job? Most wives just accept it. If the dead weight of coupledom did not obtain, wives would only accompany their husbands if it suited their purposes to do so; otherwise they would almost certainly find other ways in which to fulfil their own potential.

In a few instances husbands are now following their wives to jobs in other parts of the country, or abroad, but these are the exceptions that prove the rule. In the days when transport was arduous, communications were difficult and wives had no chance of an individual career, there was a valid reason for camp-following. Nowadays, however, when one can fly to the other side of the world in just a few hours, there is little justification for it to continue on such a large scale.

The counter-arguments can be predicted: 'But we want to keep the family together'; 'I'd be afraid that he/she might have affairs if I wasn't around'; and so on.

All these excuses stem from fear, the basis for the bondage of coupledom. People are afraid of what might happen if they do not stay with their partners at all times. They see only the negative possibilities of separation. However, if you genuinely love someone you can let him or her go. The husband or wife who pleads with the spouse not to go away for a week or so ('I can't manage without you') is displaying not love but a stifling and childish possessiveness.

People who have a lot of self-confidence and self-respect do not subscribe to the coupledom syndrome to the same degree as others. But one of the impediments to such confidence, for women, is their continuing financial dependence upon men, which means that women often have little choice but to drag around after their menfolk. If the institution of marriage were abolished – and with it the notion that one sex should be financially dependent on the other – many of the negative aspects of coupledom would vanish. People would then stay together, or be together, from pure free will, not because they would otherwise lack a roof over their heads or a steady income.

Years ago I, like most other people of my generation, saw coupledom as an unequivocally good thing. When we of the permissive generation paired up in the 'sixties, we wanted to share everything, to be together all the time. I can remember thinking that old people who slept in single beds or, worse, in single rooms, were being miserable and unloving. Now, nearly thirty years after the cosy coupledom idea well and truly set in, I can see it for what it really is – a way of suppressing individuality, of never being able to be truly yourself. If you have to be with another person all the time, in close contact, it becomes hard, eventually, to separate yourself from him or her, and to understand who you are in isolation. What happens in modern marriages and relationships is that we acquire the *habit* of coupledom, to the point where we have no idea whether we really like it or not. Like any habit, that of togetherness can become so embedded that people genuinely imagine they are not full and complete human beings unless they have a partner permanently in tow.

Whenever public personalities are interviewed, one of the first things we want to know about them is what is happening in their 'private life' – which means, are they married, are they living with somebody, are they content to be alone? When individuals become very public, journalists rush to interview their wives or husbands. Denis Thatcher has wisely remained silent since his wife became famous, refusing all interviews. Other spouses are not so coy. Kathy Botham, wife of maverick cricket genius Ian, has written her own book about their life together. When interviewed, she is never asked about herself as an individual – only about what her husband does off the cricket field. Kathy's sole interest for the public lies in the light she can shed on Ian. Being his wife, she revealed in an interview with Katharine Hadley in the *Daily Express*, has made her life so much more exciting than it would have been otherwise: 'It brings me great benefits. I meet exciting people who I get to know and like, like Elton John.'

Such is the story of a life lived at second-hand. And Kathy Botham is far from unique. One of the saddest pictures in her book, *Living with a Legend*, depicts a whole group of cricket wives sitting in the sun: why weren't they carrying on their *own* careers, playing their *own* game, building their own lives?

As a young journalist, one of my jobs used to be to interview the wives of famous sportsmen – boxers, footballers and the like. It was a deadly task. I knew and they knew that I wasn't really interested in them at all: I was there only to find out more about their husbands. If we did not all subscribe to this dreadful idea of coupledom, there would be much more freedom for each partner to pursue personal goals and ambitions. Who, deep down, wants only vicarious glory? Is this a reason for marrying, or something to be grateful for if such comes our way during a long-term relationship?

Surely true happiness comes from developing our own talents and characters. It is impossible to do this while we feel bound to

Unholy Matrimony

interact with and mirror another human being closely and continuously.

The message for the future should be autonomy and individuality – not the deadening syndrome of coupledom.

5
Why marriage is bad for women

When the American academic Jessie Bernard claimed in her famous book *The Future of Marriage* that, according to her researches, marriage made women sick and was bad for them, many 'happily married' women recoiled in horror and disbelief. Wasn't marriage supposed to be every woman's goal? Wasn't a white wedding to Mr Right the ultimate goal and ambition of every little girl? Wasn't marriage woman's natural career, for which she would willingly give up all her own personal ambitions?

Dr Bernard's book appeared in 1973, causing shock waves among women the world over. Some of us conceded that marriage had been bad for women in the dim and distant past, but had the situation not changed? Was it not possible to be free, equal and loving partners, no longer cowed and dependent? It seemed to most of us who had been brought up in the 'fifties and 'sixties that the bad old days of marriage, at least for Western women, were over, and that we could now look forward to a new age of idyllic marriages based on free choice and free love – a promise of happiness ever after.

But then we thought a bit more about what Dr Bernard had said and realized with a sinking heart that it was true. Even in the 1970s marriage gave women as bad a deal as it had ever done. Granted, there had been some reforms, major ones, and divorce was getting easier all the time: at least there was no longer any need to stay with a dreadful husband. Contraception was more reliable than at any time hitherto and it was in theory possible for women to earn their own living at last, so that keeping a roof over our heads was suddenly less problematic.

Unholy Matrimony

Otherwise, marriage has not changed nearly so much for women as we would like to think it has. Although the reforms have been considerable and the basic premise of marriage has undergone considerable change since the Middle Ages, the idea of ownership (of the wife) still prevails. We may serve our sentences in an open prison rather than a solitary confinement cell, and there may be a possibility of our getting parole, or a transfer to another prison, but marriage is still not freedom.

Those women who have been 'reclaiming' women's history have been depressed at the way nothing really changes. We may assume that anti-marriage feelings are quite new, a product of the late twentieth century when at last the possibility of financial independence through our own efforts created a reasonable alternative to marriage for women. But this is not the case. Almost ever since women have been allowed to learn to read and write, they have been railing against marriage. Even as early as the seventeenth century, some brave outspoken women were voicing the heretical notion that marriage might not be all it was made out to be by the Church and the state – an institution which was almost a holy calling, and which was honourable and right in the eyes of God.

In fact, subversive women of two or three hundred years ago were saying all the same things about marriage that its opponents say today. Even as early as 1640 there was a popular feminist rhyme which said:

> We will not be wives
> And tie up our lives
> In villainous slavery.

And in 1703 Lady Chudleigh wrote:

> Wife and servant are the same
> But only differ in the name . . .
> Then shun, oh shun, that wretched state
> And all the fawning flatterers hate.
> Value yourselves and men despise,
> You must be proud if you'll be wise.

A well-known feminist, Mary Astell, wrote in 1706 *à propos* of

Why marriage is bad for women

marriage that women did not really have a free choice in the matter. 'A woman,' she said, 'cannot properly be said to choose. All that is allowed her is to refuse or accept what is offered.' Almost all feminists of the early eighteenth century, when the women's movement had its first flowering, noted with sadness that most women had very little option in their lives but to marry somebody – simply to provide themselves with a livelihood, if nothing else.

In his book on the English marriage, Lawrence Stone notes that radical feminist statements such as these died a 'swift and natural death' and were replaced by women writers in magazines saying such things as: 'I believe that a husband has a divine right to the absolute obedience of his wife in all cases where the first duties [presumably religious] do not interfere' (this from a Mrs Hester Chapone writing in the mid-eighteenth century).

Feminism, as many modern feminists have noted, keeps dying down and being replaced by a return to the traditional belief that a wife should accept the authority of her husband and be content with this – or, in other words, make a virtue out of a necessity. For while the eighteenth-century feminists might rail and rant and rave against the institution of marriage, the sheer weight of prejudice, religious belief and convention repeatedly ensured that their words were buried, ignored or forgotten. Even today, there are signs that the brave feminism of the 'seventies is being replaced by something more traditional. A recent issue of *Harpers and Queen* devoted itself to the subject of young motherhood, and pictured wives in their very early twenties all holding babies. There is always a deviation towards the norm, or what society has established as the norm, and in reality those who rise up and rebel against it are very few – even if, as Jessie Bernard maintains, it makes them sick.

The feminist arguments against marriage are, first of all, that historically marriage has meant little more than slavery to the average woman. As marriage laws became codified, women lost all their rights. The wonder is that they did not seem to mind. It appears that hardly any women noticed that, on marriage, they were signing away all their rights to own property, to an individual income and individual status. Increasingly, from the sixteenth century onwards, husbands and wives became one in law, and that 'one' was the husband. His status was if anything enhanced by marriage. By the nineteenth century the legal ownership and slave status of women was complete, as John Stuart Mill noted in his book *The Subjection of Women*. He was also responsible for the famous statement that women did not just have to be slaves, they had to be *willing* slaves. Lawrence Stone says that the wife had to try to make marriage a success so that the theoretical legal handicaps would have no relevance to her, and the union would be based on companionship, love and duty – all fine-sounding aspirations. The only source of a woman's power over a man was the granting or withholding of sexual favours; the latter was not usually recommended as the sexual act was seen as essential to the legal continuation of a marriage.

Every now and again a maverick woman would rise up and dispute the status quo, seeing through it for what it was. But by the nineteenth century the idea of marriage being a holy sacrament was so embedded in society's consciousness that few even considered that it could all be a dastardly plot to keep women in their place, that of 'happy slaves'.

Whenever a book was published that spoke out against marriage, several others would appear within the year claiming that marriage was a woman's only true fulfilment and that she should not look for personal satisfaction; she should be content, such books declared, to find satisfaction in the home, in making her husband and children happy and comfortable and ministering to all their needs, without ever considering her own. For a long time, as the feminist writer Ann Oakley has noted, it was assumed that it was part of the female character to want to love, give and nurture. Perhaps some women might be like that, but we are not all the same. The traditional idea of marriage required all women to be exactly alike.

The most the average women could do by way of rebellion was to faint or to have hysterics, or to become a permanent invalid, retreating into a world of her own. This has not finally faded. In his disturbing play *Woman in Mind* Alan Ayckbourn portrays a woman who has bought the traditional package – marriage, subjection to husband's needs and so on – but increasingly lives in a fantasy world where people minister to her instead, and in which she is a celebrity, a successful novelist. Gradually she descends into madness, an exit route for women in both the past and the present. It is the only way many women know of escaping their bonds – bonds to which they have apparently submitted willingly.

Formerly, arguments against marriage had little impact on women's decision to marry; there was, after all, little else a woman could do, while there was a great deal of prejudice against the spinster. A woman who was not married was not seen as a 'real' woman. Until very recently, there was indeed far more status for a woman in being married than in being single, and that status was graced by a special title – 'Mrs'. Those who imagine that feminism has made great strides will find it a sobering experience to look in the social pages of *The Tatler* or *Harpers and Queen*, where they will discover that all married women are called by their husbands' names. Even Margaret Thatcher is Mrs Denis Thatcher, and the Princess Royal was until 1988 referred to by the additional name of 'Mrs Mark Phillips' (the Queen has apparently ordered the use of this appellation to cease). Far from married women rising up in rebellion against this anachronism, they actually welcome it.

When I asked Peter Townend, the social editor of *The Tatler*, about this he assured me that the majority of women preferred to be referred to as 'Mrs John Smith' and were actually annoyed if styled otherwise, presumably because the former appellation assured the world that they were not divorced: they still rejoiced in their marital 'status'.

Frailty, it seems, is still the name of woman.

In 1909, in a book called *Marriage as a Trade*, Cicely Hamilton expounded all the contemporary arguments against marriage. She observed that women on the whole had very little choice as to whether to marry or not, a situation that threatened to render them less than whole human beings. Marriage was simply an economic necessity for most women, and the only 'profession' for which they had any training. They had to marry, because they had no other means of support. Yet Cicely Hamilton was at pains to point out that she did not oppose marriage on principle:

I have no intention of attacking the institution of marriage in itself – the life companionship of a man and a woman; I merely wish to point out that there are grave disadvantages attaching to the institution as it exists today. These disadvantages I believe to be largely unnecessary and avoidable; but at present they are very real, and the results produced by them are anything but favourable to the mental, physical and moral development of woman.

Men, she went on to say, assumed that women were incomplete without them; without a man, a woman could hardly be said to exist at all. And for an unmarried woman the problems of where to live, how to eat and how to survive in the world were critical, simply because women were unlikely to have any money of their own or any individual means of support.

'My view,' wrote Cicely Hamilton, 'is that marriage for women has always been not only a trade, but a trade that is practically compulsory.' Most girls, she said, were brought up with the idea that a woman's role was to be a parasite and because women had no economic independence they had no power of refusal. They simply had no bargaining power. Although woman's only profession was marriage, said Hamilton, she could not even bargain for the best male, because the advances could only come from the man. All she could do was to dress prettily, smile sweetly and hope that some agreeable, rich, kind man would want to marry her and keep her in reasonable comfort.

Hamilton also observed that many of the so-called feminine wiles had at their root hard commercial instincts. Women had to use whatever means lay at their disposal to try to ensnare the best possible man, and if necessary to be artificial, in case their real characters were not to men's liking. So they had to be more passive than their true inclinations might have led them to be – to smile and acquiesce, to look pleased and say nothing. The habit of being passive, smiling and nurturant was, according to Hamilton, bred into women, to the extent that some women surely no longer knew who they were or what their true characters might

Why marriage is bad for women

be. Their true selves were buried under layer upon layer of artifice in accordance with the requirements of society's conventions.

This meant that few women could develop their talents or potential. Their brains were arrested at a childish stage and rarely grew beyond it. As their bodies were once constrained in whalebone corsets, so were their minds similarly constricted. This phenomenon, claims Hamilton, was brought about by sheer dependence: 'the economic need of women [forced them] to arrest their mental growth.' And of course it pleased men, enabling them to be reflected at twice their natural stature, as Virginia Woolf later pointed out. 'The ordinary male ideal of a wife is a servile ideal,' wrote Cicely Hamilton, adding that for the average man the perfect wife was 'a person with less brains than himself, who is pleasant to look at, makes him comfortable at home and respects his authority'. Women's apparent stupidity was also 'imposed upon them by need'. She also noted that women, once married, tended to undergo rapid mental deterioration – virtually to stagnate.

If only this depressing syndrome, described at the turn of the century, had become as outdated as the bustle and the penny-farthing. Unfortunately it is all too common, in the late 1980s, to see once-clever and independent married women sinking into stagnation, trapped in tedious partnerships because they imagine themselves happier and more secure as part of a couple, no matter how bad the relationship. Women are still putting themselves mentally and emotionally into whalebone corsets. We can see it happening daily – and publicly, in the case of politicians' wives and 'corporate' wives who follow their husbands around everywhere.

Although marriage is a trade, according to Cicely Hamilton, being proficient at it is no guarantee of a good livelihood. In fact, the opposite prevails. A good wife may be seen as a person who is competent at housework, child care, cooking, sewing and knitting. Yet the women who spend most time toiling at these wifely tasks are usually the poorest in our society. 'Those who work the hardest,' reflected Cicely Hamilton, 'are rewarded the

Unholy Matrimony

least.' Rich women – that is, women who marry rich men – hardly have to do these jobs at all, as they can employ staff. Cicely Hamilton wondered why it was seen as natural that women should be proficient at so many disagreeable tasks. 'Does the average man really believe,' she asked, 'that she [a woman] has an instinctive and unquenchable craving for all the unpleasant and unremunerative jobs?' The duties normally assigned to a wife were the ones the average husband would prefer not to perform.

Commenting on women's ability to reproduce their own kind, Hamilton observed drily: 'It is not upon the performance of a purely animal function that a human being should find his or her title to respect; if a woman is revered only because she reproduces her kind, a still higher reverence is due to a rabbit.'

In our own time, of course, we have extolled childbirth to an even higher degree than people did in the past. We commonly regard childbirth as a wonderful and emotionally uplifting experience, rather than something which women do as a matter of course. In the 'eighties there seems to be a conspiracy to force women into their so-called 'natural' role. It is still assumed that every woman will want to reproduce her own kind and, in order to do so, be content to be dependent upon a male partner. Far from emancipating women from their dependence upon forming an exclusive partnership, we dragoon them into it.

Women, as we have repeatedly been told, want to love above everything. Such is the received wisdom. But do they? We commonly assume that women are the ones who will give up all for love, without even noticing the sacrifice. If that is so, where are the great love poems written by women?

In the conclusion to her book, Cicely Hamilton reminds us:

For all that love is her whole existence, no woman has ever sung of love as man has sung of it, has painted it, has embodied it in drama.

When she is in love, a woman can only repeat what men have said on the subject, and appropriate it to herself. Cicely Hamilton had a point: most women have nothing original to say on the subject of love – perhaps because, after all, they do not feel it as powerfully as men do.

Almost two decades after this book appeared the novelist Charlotte Haldane wrote a book defending marriage. She restated the conventional notion that it was normal for a woman to be married, and abnormal to be anything else. If marriage fell into disrepute, warned Haldane, the family and the home would also completely disintegrate, and then where would we be?

The notions of marriage and the position of women which obtained from the late nineteenth century to the 1930s are analysed in a book by Sheila Jeffreys, *The Spinster and Her Enemies*. Jeffreys, a lesbian feminist and, as such, vehemently opposed to heterosexual, patriarchal marriage, maintains in her book that women who were not married commonly used to be seen as 'superfluous' or 'spare' and 'a problem'. The idea that 'spare' women might be able to lead fulfilling lives on their own without being tied to a man was unthinkable. Jeffreys says that women who fail to relate to men are still encountering social disdain, even today, so strong is the convention that we must move in male/female indissoluble units.

Many feminists of the nineteenth century argued forcefully against marriage. These women included such immortal heroines as Florence Nightingale and Christabel Pankhurst, who both saw marriage as annihilation for women. What killed the feminist movement of the time, according to Sheila Jeffreys, was the notion that heterosexual intercourse was fundamentally necessary to a woman's well-being – to her psychic and emotional as well as her physical health. Once the sexologists got to work, women themselves became ardent campaigners for sexual liberation and gained the licence to enjoy, rather than simply endure, a sexual relationship with a man who was preferably a husband. Sex, heterosexual love and motherhood were glorified. Those women who condemned sex as the assertion of male domination were effectively silenced by the new debate claiming sexual fulfilment for women.

In Jeffreys' view, all through the nineteenth and early twentieth centuries women were seeking and finding fulfilling relationships with members of their own gender. But from the 1920s onwards, when the ideas of people such as Havelock Ellis

Unholy Matrimony

were disseminated – often by eager and willing female disciples – the premise that a woman could be happy on her own, without a man, fell into disrepute. Women then began to feel, says Jeffreys, that they had freely chosen the subordinate roles of wife, mother and dependant – as, indeed, so many still do. 'Spinsterhood,' she writes, 'became associated with sterility, destructiveness and anti-life.'

The eroticizing of married women, Jeffreys tells us, was the greatest sociological change of the 1920s. Before that, women had been allowed not to like sex and not to be regarded as sexual beings. Suddenly, all women were sex objects and all were presumed to take an interest in sex for its own sake. The net result was to make women more dependent upon men than ever, because, according to the received wisdom of the day, their health and well-being depended on sexual satisfaction. The arch exponent of this idea was Marie Stopes.

Sex became the new binding ingredient for a happy marriage after the Married Women's Property Act and certain divorce law reforms had made it slightly easier for women to escape. What has happened in marriage, as Jeffreys so rightly observes, is that one form of dependence and domination has simply been substituted for another. No sooner does society enact some liberating laws than it imprisons those it has liberated with another set of constraints. Only the chains change.

Sheila Jeffreys quotes a comment made at the Sex Reform Congress in 1929 by Joanna Elberskircher:

Patriarchal marriage and civilization were attained at the cost of the prostitution of all womankind and women were brought up to be victims . . . [Man] robs her of her natural rights, her right to determine her own life, her freedom of choice, her right to work . . . Her economic existence, indeed her whole existence, is now based fundamentally on her sexual function and on her sexual relation to the male.

When this speech was made, marriage was enjoying a greater popularity than almost ever before. In fact, its popularity has grown throughout the twentieth century. In past ages, the unmarried constituted a larger proportion of society; in the eighteenth century, for example, one in ten 50-year-olds were still unmarried, and 8-15 per cent of all women were unmarried. Servants, governesses, the religious and academics were often among those who did not marry, and the maiden aunt and bachelor uncle seemed to be a more common phenomenon than they are today. According to Jeffreys, the modern notion that everybody has to be married, if they are to be considered normal, first became widespread after the First World War.

She writes:

After World War One, despite an increased 'surplus' of women over men, the popularity of marriage and the rate of marriage increased steadily. Every possibility was used to strengthen the basic heterosexual relationship. Sexual intercourse was seen to be necessary for the welding together of married couples in a way it never had been in the nineteenth century.

The idea grew up, says Jeffreys, that sexual intercourse was a basic necessity of everyday life, and there was a 'massive campaign' to conscript women into enthusiastic participation in sex. There were attempts, she writes, to 'therapize women into enjoyment' of it.

All through the 1920s, she writes, the role of women was constantly being narrowed to that of complementing men in the act of sexual intercourse. Jeffreys finishes her account by saying that aggressive male sexuality is now the organizing principle of the universe.

Although the late nineteenth century had seen a long overdue flowering of possibilities for women in education and, to a lesser extent, careers, with the founding of colleges at Oxford and Cambridge and the opening up of the nursing profession, women were still brought up to believe that marriage was what they should really want, and for which they should be prepared to give up their education, their talents and their capacity for making an independent living.

Women had it drummed into them, by other women as much as by men, that they should consider their education and career worthily sacrificed for 'love', that they should be happy to trade in their independence for dependence and would never regret it.

This belief has by no means vanished. Even today, all too many women are prepared to give up their careers to follow their men about, or to produce children. But why? Why should any woman consider another person's life more important than her own?

I believe that there are forces at work which are more powerful than mere social constructs. I believe that there is an inherent weakness in women which makes them continue to want to marry – a weakness which can hardly be touched by feminism or sisterhood. It is the weakness of attachment and dependence, the feeling that unless we are 'completed' by one other special person, we are not really whole human beings. We commonly call this frailty 'falling in love', or being ruled by one's heart rather than one's head, and it happens as commonly with lesbians as it does with heterosexual women. Men have parallel but not quite identical weaknesses, and it is these which make *them* want to marry. Such weakness – on the part of both sexes – makes us still believe, against all the evidence, that marriage is the only proper way to relate to other people.

Nowadays there is no logical need for people to marry. Both men and women can exist independently, earn their own living, buy houses and obtain all the services available from the state. No woman actually needs a man in order to survive. Nor does any man need a woman for survival.

We do not even need a sexual relationship for reproductive purposes any more. Nowadays, it is easy to reproduce by means of insemination by donor. Sperm banks and clinics where this service can be obtained are now relatively common. It is also very easy to self-inseminate, as growing numbers of women are finding. In the book *Having a Baby Without a Man* (1986) it is estimated that about 16,000 single women per year are now deciding to reproduce in this way in the USA. Dr Robert Snowdon, director of the Centre for Population Research at Exeter University, has interviewed many single and lesbian mothers who have had children by AID (artificial insemination by donor). He says that there is no doubt that these are the most loved, wanted and well cared for children he has ever come across. Women who choose to reproduce by alternative insemination are those who do not want any kind of relationship with a man, nor do they want him to play a part in the upbringing of their children. Sperm donors are regarded in much the same way as blood donors – as providing a service, rather than being fathers.

I predict that the ability of women to have children without involving a man, except for the anonymous donation of sperm, is going to have profound and far-reaching effects on our ideas of marriage and the family. There is no evidence to suggest that children of single parents, whose mothers have freely chosen such a method of conception, suffer in any way in comparison with those conceived by conventional methods within traditional two-parent families. The question of children is more fully discussed in Chapter 8.

According to the marriage service in the *Book of Common Prayer*, marriage was ordained primarily for the procreation of children. But it is patently not necessary for marriage to precede the advent of children. Nor are they any longer the primary reason for people marrying.

We marry quite simply because we believe that by doing so we shall become happier. The fact that we usually become miserable instead does not seem to make any difference.

But marriages which are undertaken for 'happiness' have no more chance of success – probably less – than those which used to be contracted from grim necessity. Although thousands of women recognized the truth of what Jessie Bernard was saying in her book *The Future of Marriage* (1973), it has not stopped us from rushing into that state, as enthusiastically as ever – if not more so.

Jessie Bernard argues that marriage laws are always based on male conceptions, the premise that women were created for men rather than the other way round. As a 'helpmeet', a wife is traditionally not entitled to payment for housework, and her earnings have until recently been virtually under her husband's control.

Women, Jessie Bernard says, very often maintain that their marriages are happy: after all, they initially married with the intention of increasing their happiness. Also, many women cannot see a valid alternative, so they suppose they must be happy, even though they do not actually feel happy. It is their health, Bernard says, which gives the lie to their declarations of contentment, Dr Bernard discovered that married women are far more likely than single ones to suffer from all kinds of health problems, both mental and emotional.

In particular, married women are extremely prone to depression. This, Dr Bernard concludes, is because they are stifled within marriage, even a modern kind of marriage: they are not allowed to be themselves. Women have been brought up to believe they must wangle and manipulate their men to get their own way. Such subterfuge, the only power they possess, eats away inside them, robs them of self-confidence and, after a time, the ability to act independently.

Many women spend so much time trying to please men, to anticipate their needs, to put them first and then perhaps wangle something for themselves, that they exhaust themselves in the effort. But putting someone else first is virtually impossible. How can we ever know what is right for somebody else? It is hard enough to know what is right for ourselves.

Most women brought up in the Judaeo-Christian tradition have been taught that they must put other people first and not think about themselves. Yet this is a recipe for disaster, not happiness. When women put their all into trying to please other people, they forget who they are, what they should be doing, and start to live in a twilight world where nothing is ever satisfactory. When women start living their lives on other people's terms in the belief that they are being unselfish, they often begin relying on tranquillizers and falling prey to depression. True giving and loving serve to elevate an individual, not to make him or her sink into apathy, resentment and hostility.

Jessie Bernard states what all feminists know – that marriage gives the male a superior status to the female. A husband, she says, very often is superior to his wife in height, age, education and earning ability. Indeed, men so often marry somebody slightly below them in age, education and earning ability that this is seen as perfectly normal. For example, a boss may marry his much younger secretary, a lecturer his student, a doctor a nurse. Rarely does it happen the other way round, and indeed, an older, higher-earning, tall male is still considered a 'catch' for a young woman. A young, non-earning male who is short of stature is considered no kind of catch at all.

Men traditionally want wives who are subservient and who will look up to them and believe they are better than they really are. The younger the woman, the less likely she is to be able to see the truth. A man who has never been married, says Dr Bernard, is usually considered to be at the bottom of the barrel (unless he is gay, of course) whereas an ever-single woman will very often be a high achiever.

The less well adjusted, well educated and mature a women is, according to Bernard, the more appeal marriage will have for her. This is certainly true. Magazines aimed at the barely-literate girl are full of 'love stories' and posters of hunky pop stars. The advice columns and fashion articles also reflect the universal goal of getting one's man – as if this were the only achievement of which readers are capable. The message of the teen magazines is as avidly consumed in the late 1980s as it ever was.

The trouble is that even the dimmest and least mature girl very soon learns that men are not as strong and dependable as she hoped. They are by no means the forceful romantic heroes depicted in the magazines. Few are like the rock stars, earning piles of money and always looking cool and in control. It does not take the average girl long to find out that this man she has married, though possibly quite pleasant, is nothing special and cannot do what she most hoped he would – make her happy. She has been fooled by the stereotypes, Bernard tells us. At the same time her legal status has been considerably lowered by her marriage and she has become a non-person. She has given up so much and gained so little. No wonder by the time she is 30 she is likely to have spent hours in the doctor's surgery queuing for tranquillizers.

Jessie Bernard claims that after marriage women become more submissive and dependent than they were before. After fifteen or twenty years of marriage the majority have become completely helpless, unable to do the simplest tasks on their own. One woman revealed in an article in *The Independent* that whereas before marriage she had hiked round the world alone with a backpack, now she almost had to phone her husband at his office to ask if she should wash her hair. The writer of this article asserted that financial dependence had brought her to this sorry state. In fact it goes deeper than this, because even high-earning women can become helpless within marriage. It happens because the very institution of marriage encourages dependence in women, and in time this becomes a habit that is hard to break.

Dr Bernard writes: 'Women have an increasingly negative and passive outlook in time.' Housework causes the mind to deteriorate and the isolation experienced by many women in the home also has a negative effect. There is no solidarity in housewifehood, which is why it is so debilitating a condition. The isolation encourages brooding, leads to erratic judgements and makes women more susceptible to psychosis. In isolation, a woman's sense of powerlessness and hopelessness grows almost daily.

Yet in spite of all this, women continue to marry. Jessie Bernard says the main reason is the deadening pressure to conform. Because we are told so often that marriage and babies will make us happy, we grow up believing it, and have to try it for ourselves. Very, very few women can ultimately resist the pressure, even if they hold out for a few years.

There is, as many of us realize, a conspiracy not to tell the truth about marriage. Most of us grow up in homes where our parents are patently not happy with each other. Where there should be laughter, tolerance and friendliness, there are often bitterness and resentment, perhaps seething underneath the surface. Yet we are led to believe that, given a little work, a little give and take, this marriage could have been happy; or, even if it could not, it just meant that these particular people were married to the wrong partners. Very few women are brought up to believe that it is marriage itself which is bad. So we all grow up imagining, hoping and believing that our marriages will be different, and that the awfulness which prevailed in our childhood homes will not be a factor in our own establishments.

Dr Bernard believes that when women say they are happy in their marriages they in fact mean that they have adjusted to them. She says that women are 'deformed' to fit them for marriage. Their motivational wings are cut and their intellectual feet are bound. Girls have been shaped since birth for dependency and passivity and imagine that this is their individual character, when in fact it is an imposed ideal.

Jessie Bernard writes:

Women need and want the love and companionship and the mere presence of men in some kind of close relationship. They demonstrate this need by clinging to marriage regardless of the cost. They are willing to pay dearly for it. This fact assures its future.

The basic message from Jessie Bernard is that marriage is bad for women because it cuts them off from living a full life of their own and makes them imagine that the only power they can have is vicarious, or that they will themselves become powerful by aligning themselves with a man who is. What happens instead is a slow and painful realization that marriage means powerlessness and lack of status for women. Although very many women maintain they are happy to be wives and mothers and that thereby they find their fulfilment, their mental, emotional and physical health does not bear this out. Marriage takes away what a woman has, rather than bestowing anything extra. In the past, most women who achieved either had to stay single or achieve *in spite* of their marriage, not because of it. Many are the women who wrote novels or painted in secret, in case their husbands found out that they had been doing something on their own. This situation prevails even today. Many creative women have felt it their duty to stop playing the piano, painting or whatever in order to be a 'proper' wife and support their husbands.

Jessie Bernard draws attention to the fallacy that some men's success in business has depended on the support services provided by their wives – as secretaries, typists, editors, accountants or other types of functionary. But although no man's success in the outside world depends on his *wife*, as opposed to any other person, performing these tasks, still the popular myth prevails.

Looking around us, we can see for ourselves that wifehood confers no real status. Feminists for two hundred years or more have been telling us that marriage is bad for women. The facts are incontrovertible. Marriage endangers women's health and renders them half-people: incomplete, fearful, timid, phobic.

So why is marriage still so popular? Why have we not voted with our feet and decided we will have nothing to do with it? And why, even if we divorce, do we rush to remarry?

The answer is that we marry – both men and women – largely through fear. We may claim to marry for love, for commitment, for many fine-sounding reasons, but in reality we come together through fear. We are afraid of being alone, unwanted and unloved, and we imagine, in our fear, that the way not to be alone and unloved is to join ourselves with another person in a permanent union. Friendship is not enough: a legally binding arrangement, sanctioned by Church and state, is the only one we believe will do.

Now that marriage has lost its practical value in our society, it has acquired a far more insidious function. It is a way of ensuring that each of us will be able to exist as part of a loving twosome.

Ann Oakley tussles with the subject of love and what being part of a loving twosome can do to a woman in her honest autobiography *Taking It Like a Woman*. She voices the dilemma which many, if not most, women have had to face when they experience feelings commonly considered part of the package generally known as 'falling in love':

The problem [of giving into love] is feeling too much. Let me analyse it, because it is a female problem and therefore not mine alone: it is, moreover, a problem of love, of all the love stories that happen between men and women. In it is wrapped up the doggedness of dependence, the need for one human being to be affected by another. How can any of us love without dependence, without laying ourselves open to the most horrendous conflicts and disasters?

We cannot, because we grow up believing that dependence, or

at least, interdependence, is a good thing — and therein lie almost all of our difficulties.

Oakley continues:

As a woman, in the first place, my emotions rule my life. From them I derive the pleasure and the pain of my existence. My thoughts are directed by them. There is nothing that I do or think which is not inspired by feelings.

In the second place, I take it as my chief duty to study the feelings of others. Their emotional welfare is my concern.

In the third place, any attachment that is formed between myself and another becomes, for its duration, my ruling concern. I become inseparable from that person, and lose much of my capacity for independent voluntary action. I have given myself up to the other person, whether or not such self-sacrifice was asked for and I am, indeed, nearly willing to give up everything.

Ann Oakley asserts that women who create the 'security of the family' knowing that they are creating their own prison can ultimately do without it. She summarizes the process by saying, 'You begin by sinking into his arms and end up with your arms in his sink.'

What should concern us as a human community is how to form loving, lasting, reproductive relationships which bestow freedom instead of confinement. But the trouble is that we are confined by our emotions. It is this very capacity for feeling, and our delusion that attachment and dependence are positive emotions, which lead us into a prison from which it is difficult to escape. The problem is not so much that women are confined by men in high-security jails, as that we are kept there because our minds imprison us.

It seems that there is no way of creating the loving, lasting relationships Ann Oakley longs for while at the same time preserving freedom. You can have one or the other. As the seventeenth-century hymn has it, the only truly free person is an individual 'whose passions not his masters are'. Modern society has come to see it as ennobling to be enslaved by emotions and we have graced the negative emotion of wanting to bind another to us with the name of love. The most constricting straitjacket is the one which we create for ourselves.

When people 'fall in love' they lose, temporarily, the capacity for independent thought and action. Unfortunately, by the time this ability is regained, they have often reached the point of no return. Once love has gone, they have to pretend they have freely chosen their prison, that it is the place where they can be happiest, and that they would not want to be on their own again. If they do not pretend, life becomes intolerable.

Ann Oakley has had the honesty to face up to the contradictions and problems inherent in our desire for love and that one special person. She knows it takes away from us, rather than giving us something worth having, and yet, as we all know, it is very seductive and can seem wonderful for a time. So, of course, can any addictive substance or activity – heroin, alcohol, gambling. All deliver wonderful short-term benefits: if they did not, would people continue to be hooked? We are addicted to wanting to be in love and, for women as well as men, it is the prime cause of our downfall.

Mary Daly, in her famous feminist 'bibles' *Gyn/Ecology* and *Pure Lust*, has observed how women easily become token torturers of other women, carrying out cruel and restrictive practices to confine other women's lives. It is other women, she says, who in the past bound the feet of little girls in China. It is other women who carry out female circumcision in the Middle East. Men have no part in these mutilations and stay far away while they are being carried out.

In the societies Mary Daly analyses, little boys do not undergo similar mutilations. The purpose of foot-binding and circumcision is to fit and adapt little girls for marriage, to make them more compliant, more 'feminine', and hence better wives.

We like to imagine that these horrors have all disappeared. But in fact they have only been replaced. The trouble is that when a custom is current, we tend to accept it without a second thought. A few years ago I wrote an article in *The Times* saying that I considered it humiliating and degrading that wives should accompany their husbands on business trips. By implication, I also made it clear that I considered it wrong for wives to follow their husbands round the world simply because of their husbands' careers. Later I did a radio broadcast on the same theme.

I was astonished and saddened by the amount of hate mail my views provoked. Not one woman who wrote to me agreed with me. I was accused of rocking the very foundations of marriage by suggesting that wives should not accompany husbands; that their place was not necessarily by their husbands' side. Many wives wrote to tell me how they felt their lives had been enhanced by trips within their own country or abroad, made courtesy of their spouse's company.

In a *Daily Telegraph* article on the wives of diplomats, Catherine Stott writes:

> No one promotes the image of the stiff British upper lip more successfully than the pragmatic members of our own diplomatic service and their staunchly supportive wives.

The article highlighted the problems encountered by these staunchly supportive wives when they wipe themselves out of existence to go and be supportive in a foreign country, and how the younger women are beginning to assert themselves and rebel. Some of them have in fact refused to accompany their husbands abroad. In recogniton of the new mood among incoming Foreign Office wives there are now moves to make them more content with their second-hand existence – job opportunities, increased status and fuller lives of their own.

The wind of change has started to blow through the serried ranks of female incorporation, where a wife has no independence and is only in a particular place by virtue of her husband's job. But instead of rethinking the whole idea of coupledom and wifely duty, attention is now being directed to how wives can still go abroad and not mind. The rebelliousness is being crushed at once in order to prevent the status quo being undermined by wives getting above themselves.

Again, inevitably, it is the wives of longer standing, the ones who camp-followed without a murmur, who are trying to persuade the new 'intake' to do the same. After all, they would hate to feel their own lives had been thrown away and that they had achieved precisely nothing. The magazine of the Diplomatic Service Wives' Association is all for younger wives fitting in – having their feet bound, as it were. Its editor's policies were outlined in a recent *Daily Telegraph* feature:

There is lots of training in London in portable skills you can use abroad. Doctors and nurses could work if there was some agreement within the FO. Many of the jobs at each mission done by local staff could be done by wives if there was some central training scheme . . . I worry that the young wives coming in now have less patience and less inclination to go abroad . . . People at the top must respond to what these women are saying, or in twenty years' time you could reach a situation where wives don't want to go abroad. And without this, the Foreign Office isn't going to be effective.

The proposal, predictably, is to crush the women's rebellion by allowing a few small reforms to keep them happy. There is, however, no question of either the men or the Foreign Office adapting and changing the very basis of postings abroad. Wives really do not count, and never have.

As Hilary Callan and Shirley Ardener say in their deeply researched book *The Incorporated Wife*, the only impact a wife ever has in a foreign posting – if she has any at all – is negative. She is seen as a nuisance if she asserts herself, wants a job abroad or refuses to go with her husband. The husband is never seen as a nuisance if he asserts *his* wish to take one of these postings. Wives who have adapted themselves so well that one hardly notices they are there are the 'successful' ones. The only answer is somehow to school assertive women into obedience and acceptance. And the best people to do this, of course, are other women. If other women can tell the rebellious wives that their job is to be with their husbands, and that by being there they will be doing their bit for their country, there is likely to be more acceptance and acquiescence than if the men were to try to dragoon them.

In the army, too, other women are being used to persuade wives that they can be happy if they move about every two years or so with their husbands. (The army is so liberated in its attitude

Why marriage is bad for women

to women that until recently it was policy to address a woman as 'wife of', and husbands even had to sign their wives' library cards.) One Colonel Michael Gaffney was apparently so alarmed by the numbers of young soldiers leaving the service because their wives would not accompany them abroad that he commissioned a report on army wives. This covered 75,000 of them and resulted in Fred, a computerized service that is to help wives find jobs abroad for themselves. The computer, run by the Federation of Army Wives (another organization that uses women to keep other women in their place), logs suitable vacancies in foreign fields. *The Sunday Times* reported that one of the first wives to 'benefit' from the service is a 27-year-old languages graduate whose husband is an army cook. She must be deeply thrilled by the knowledge that she can take a little job abroad. The computer service means that marriages can be kept together because wives, having found themselves something to do with their time overseas, will not become bored and turn to alcohol when their husbands are not around.

The wife who set up the computer project is however relinquishing the task – because she is about to follow her husband to his new post at Osnabruck. The more things change, the more they stay the same. If only the stranglehold of coupledom did not persist, there would be no need for computers like Fred. And if only people did not 'fall in love' the problem of wives accompanying husbands abroad would not arise either. With friendship rather than the tyranny of marital 'love', men and women could be separated for many months, even years, and each would gain by it. At present, we imagine that even a few months' separation must endanger a marriage.

Underlying this view is a fear that if we are separated from our spouses for some while we may get to like it, as so many women during the Second World War did. And that would not bode well for the future of marriage. Men, also separated from their wives, might enjoy their new freedom too – not just to go off with other women, but to be themselves, freed from the constraints of the confining marital relationship.

Many of my friends are currently uncomfortable within their

marriages. Having belatedly become aware of feminism, they realize that they have sold out, lived their lives to no personal purpose, and now feel sick at heart. Should they 'give up' everything they have worked for – the smart interlined curtains, the floodlit garden, the tennis court and the paddock, artefacts largely acquired with their husbands' money? Or should they soldier on and try to change the basis of their relationship? When the husbands get wind of this, as eventually they must, instead of meeting the arguments head on and sorting them out fairly, they invite other, more docile women to dinner so that they can put the erring wife fully back in her place. The message is: 'I'm happy with my husband and what he gives me: so should you be.' Thus husbands get other women to do their dirty work for them.

Women are token torturers still. Instead of leading our own lives and pursuing our own careers, we are still lamely following the man's lead, and many of us try to dragoon other women into doing the same, willingly and lovingly. It is largely other women who try to persuade the 'rebels' to conform, accept their lot and neither question nor complain. Women are often fond of telling other women that their greatest chance of happiness lies in a close relationship with a man who can support them financially and to whom they can look up. They proudly call themselves 'Mrs John Smith', never challenging the convention or asking themselves whether any man would call himself 'Mr Jane Smith' where Smith is the wife's maiden name. Thus convention holds sway – the old convention which has always militated against women's individuality.

All over the world educated women relinquish their independence in the belief that their husbands and children 'need' a woman to be constantly in the home. In a series of letters that appeared recently in *The Spectator* on the question of child benefit, currently paid to every woman in the UK with a dependent child, women correspondents claimed that this money was their 'only independence'. Child benefit amounts to just over £7 per week per child. What kind of 'independence' can a woman have on that? Even on social security and without the 'protection' of a man, she would immediately be far better off, financially as well as emotionally. How could the (highly educated) women who wrote these letters be so pathetic as not to realize the absurdity of their situation?

It is hard to understand how, now that there is a choice, so many women can cut off their source of financial independence to become a slave, a servant, a parasite. And yet many do, truly believing they are doing something noble and fine in 'giving up' their careers to bring up children or to 'support' a man emotionally and domestically. The more women continue to do this, the more they will encourage other women to do the same. A daughter who sees her mother fussing around her father will grow up believing this is the natural thing to do even though she hears her mother complaining of her lot – the drudgery of housework, the lack of opportunity to get out of the house, the narrow horizons. For women are the great complaining sex.

Among all the married couples I know, it is the wife, not the husband, who complains. The endless complaining is an outward sign of impotence and resentment. Yet, if one of these women were suddenly to be offered an escape route, she would probably not take it. 'John needs me,' she would say. Many women are quite proud of the fact that their husbands cannot shop or cook or sew on buttons. This constitutes proof for the wives that they are needed and loved, yet in fact *any* woman, or man for that matter, could perform these tasks. You don't have to be emotionally attached to someone in order to carry them out.

Marriage has for so many centuries been seen as the only valid way for women to exist that we have blinded ourselves to its many negative sides. As soon as one reason for marriage fades away and becomes insignificant, another comes in to take its place. As women, we no longer need men to provide for us financially. Nor do we have to marry simply to have food and shelter. Nor do we even have to marry to legitimize our children – the differences between 'legitimate' and 'illegitimate' children have been almost completely eroded.

The new arguments for persuading women into marriage are based on personal and sexual fulfilment. We believe that in order to function as proper human beings we must be able to relate to

Unholy Matrimony

another human in an intimate and exclusive partnership, and are widely judged on our ability to stick to another person, to 'stand by' our partner. Since the advent of AIDS the idea of traditional marriage has been advocated even more strongly than it was throughout the 'sixties and 'seventies. All the traditionalists are now declaring in triumph, 'God meant us to be married and to stick to just one partner. Otherwise, why did he send us, in his infinite wisdom, the AIDS plague?'

The AIDS scare is being employed as another weapon in the age-old battle to persuade us that marriage is best for all of us. However, the overwhelming majority of AIDS sufferers are not monogamously married people but male homosexuals, prostitutes, drug addicts and haemophiliacs. Fear of AIDS is no reason at all for any woman to accept marriage.

As feminists know, single women are often stronger, more creative, more independent and even happier than married women. That is all very well, the majority of women may say, for the few eccentrics and peculiar people like lesbians who do not want to get married, but these single-by-choice women are not the 'normal' majority. Marriage, however, *is* still the norm; it still does as much harm to women as ever it did, and yet, perversely, we try to pretend that it is not harmful, that it is basically a good institution which simply needs a little rethink, and perhaps a bit of work.

What really needs to be changed is the way in which men and women see each other; they must stop regarding each other as possessions, accept each other as individuals *and let each other remain so*. Non-intimate friendships, brother-and-sister-type relationships, are the positive way forward. But as yet we cannot or will not see it.

6
Why marriage is bad for men

Given that marriage is so patently a patriarchal institution, the world over, ordained by men for the supposed benefit of men, it might be expected that male critics of the institution are few and far between.

In fact, a number of far-sighted men have always known that any institution which disbenefits one sex can hardly enhance the other. While most men throughout history have assumed that it is in the natural order of things for males to be dominant and women to be subservient, a few have always seen that this idea is most probably a social construct and not innate or natural at all. And the most far-sighted men have always known that the institution of marriage heightens the differences between the sexes, so that each partner is artificially enhanced or diminished simply by the nature of the relationship.

The most vociferous early opponents of marriage were the founding fathers of the Christian Church. Some of the Greek philosophers may have held that marriage was a necessary evil and that the highest form of relationship was that formed between men, but marriage was nevertheless instrinsic to their society, as it was to Roman and Jewish society. The early Christians were the first to see that marriage could be extremely disbeneficial to both men and women. They claimed that the close and continuing presence of a woman inflamed male lust and made it difficult for the man to concentrate on the important task of communion with God. Many of the early Christians, those who have now been canonized as saints, believed that sexual contact with a woman was a defilement, and that women were a snare for

Unholy Matrimony

the God-fearing man. Few of them bothered to think about what marriage and close intimate contact with a man might do to a woman.

In Semitic religions, all men are urged to marry and there is no tradition of either male or female celibacy. Marriage is held to be ordained solely for the benefit of men, and women are brought up to acquiesce to this and to believe that this is the natural order of things: God's law, which no man or woman should ever attempt to contravene.

This attitude prevails in the Old Testament and is accepted by both Jews and Muslims as the word of God. Women are regarded, with only a few exceptions, as the property of men, and hardly possess even the passive power of veto.

But when Christianity came along there was at its root an idea of female equality and autonomy; certainly until the Reformation Christianity allowed an honourable alternative to marriage. This alternative still exists, of course, within Roman Catholicism: celibacy and the monastic life.

Jesus, according to Karen Armstrong in her book *The Gospel According to Woman*, himself remained indifferent to family life, even though he was a Jew brought up in the tradition of the extended family. Jesus believed and taught that family life was a distraction from communion with God and could therefore only be considered a second-best kind of existence.

Although Judaic law stated that only men could study the Scriptures, Jesus told women they had an equal right to this knowledge when, in the story of Mary and Martha, Martha fusses around serving and seeing to the catering arrangements while Mary just sits at the Lord's feet. Jesus says of Mary that she has 'chosen the better part' (*Luke* 10: 38-42).

I am indebted to Karen Armstrong for pointing out this example. Jesus' new world order, says Armstrong, 'reverses old positions, is liberating women from domestic triviality and giving them a place equal to men. Women should no longer waste their energies fussing about the catering arrangements at parties. . . To both men and women this kind of triviality is irrelevant and they should seek the one thing necessary. Again a woman's main glory is no longer motherhood, even if she is the mother of the Messiah.'

Jesus was in fact a feminist and understood, as all men of genius and insight must, that the institution of marriage, by its very nature, oppresses women.

St Paul has been held to be a woman-hater because he was against marriage, much as modern feminists are held to be man-haters when they say the same thing. But to hate an institution which imposes an unnatural and ultimately negative closeness on the partners is not the same as hating every member of the opposite sex. St Paul is commonly regarded as the arch anti-feminist because he was so against marriage, but in fact, in sanctioning an escape route, he and the other early Christians did much to free women from oppression.

Jesus and his disciples realized that the holy vocation of celibacy (as they saw it) was not and never could be for everybody, but they held it up as an ideal for those who were strong enough and self-confident enough to embrace it. As we have seen, the Church of England marriage service states at the outset that marriage is for those who 'have not the gift of continence', thus preserving a relic of that old idea. Early Christians saw marriage as a reflection of weakness. Whenever there is a valid alternative to marriage, the status of women in society is automatically upgraded. In its early days Christianity attracted a great deal of women, possibly for the very reason that it offered this alternative to being virtually sold into slavery, as otherwise happened in Roman and Jewish societies. Most women, as ever, were conditioned into docility and acceptance but there were always a few mavericks who saw that life could offer more. Many of these single-minded women became the virgin saints of the early Christian Church.

Karen Armstrong maintains that the first Christians did not value the family above all else, but saw personal autonomy as a higher ideal. From a Christian point of view, marriage was considered instrinsically bad for men because it kept their minds on earthly matters, reminded them constantly of their sensual and sexual appetites and encouraged lust. The more male lust grew,

Unholy Matrimony

according to the early Christians, the less likely it was that a man could have a proper relationship with God. Families also provided fertile ground for the other negative emotions of hate, jealousy, possessiveness, greed and envy to flourish. A man who had a family might look at another family and see that they were materially better off; wanting such comforts for himself, he might wage war on the other family and plunder their possessions. A single man, on the other hand, would be less likely to covet, and hence to steal and murder, so the theory went.

Men who had families would want more and more money and would start to worry about defending their territory, expanding it, keeping the other members of the family in order, consolidating positions and establishing a hierarchy. A man with no family, in the opinion of the early Christians, would be free from many temptations. Without the bondage of marriage and fatherhood, he would be free to become a better person. Alone, or in a monastic community, he would be encouraged to shed his vices and cultivate his virtues.

In the early Christian days and the Middle Ages the men largely responsible for the spread of learning, for the building of cathedrals all over Europe, for establishing schools and universities and for exerting a generally civilizing influence on society were monks. Celibate and pacificist by vocation, these monks also wrote poetry, translated the Bible, wrote treatises and other learned works. Their very freedom from the constraints and distractions of the family enabled them to be productive and spread the ideal of peace.

When a man does not have a family, he is unlikely to be warlike, because families and dynasties, and the perceived need to protect them, are what originally caused men to wage war against each other. One of the most famous wars in history, the Trojan War, was over a woman. Lives were lost and cities ransacked, just because one man wanted a woman who had already been appropriated by another man. Wars are usually waged to regain or appropriate property of one kind or another, and war-like traits tend to emerge when a man has a family.

In Christianity, says Armstrong, the ideal of female independence has existed for 2,000 years, simply because marriage has never been seen as the only way for a woman to conduct her life. Marriage and dependence go hand in hand, for men as well as for women. Men are equally dependent – but the outcome is different from that of female dependence. The early Christians knew that the way to autonomy and independence was to keep oneself free from intimate, long-lasting unions. For hundreds of years, the highest ideal among Christians of both genders was no marriage and no sex, ever. Once a person married, they understood, autonomy was lost as the partners became bound up with each other's wishes and preferences.

Whenever a particular society sees marriage as at most a second-best way to live one's life, the status of women is automatically upgraded and the sexes have far more respect for each other than when they are conjoined forever by law. Christianity saw that a union such as marriage, which brought men and women into inevitably close contact with each other, was likely to contaminate them both. Instead of increasing strengths, as some might imagine, marriage in fact compounds weaknesses.

Within marriage women are liable to become dependent, cringing, manipulative and wily. Men are liable to become bullies, overpowering, dominant and quick to show anger. Marriage tends to bring out the worst in both sexes – dependence and passivity in women, arrogance and aggressiveness in men. Even weak and vacillating men can become domineering in their marriages. Both sexes start to feed off each other's weaknesses and unconsciously encourage and stimulate them. Many divorced men and women have said that parts of their character which had been hidden or suppressed for years suddenly emerged on their becoming single again. It was as if they had been half-people during their marriages, expecting the other person to 'complete' them.

The pioneer Christians knew this, which was why they offered an alternative to marriage. As peace-loving people they knew that the fewer the marriages, the less likelihood there was of war: those who have neither wife nor family do not have the same need for property and territory as those who do. Also, men who were not

Unholy Matrimony

married were less likely to develop a false sense of their own superiority.

As women are physically weaker than men and until recently were unable to protect themselves from the risk of pregnancy, they have always been conditioned to be afraid of men. They realized or were brought up to believe that men could easily overpower them and dominate them. Mingled with this fear was the feeling that they had to have a man to look after them because they could not possibly look after themselves. Yet, paradoxically, if they did not allow men an intimate position in their lives, they found they had no need to be afraid of them. It is only through marriage that men and women become afraid of one another and develop strategies for coping with that fear. Women traditionally become timid and passive, while men become dominant and angry.

In marriage, most men soon begin to see that they can have the upper hand, which usually encourages the worst side of their natures to assert itself. Traditionally, men have treated their wives badly – not as equals, not with respect, but as possessions, inferiors, slaves they can kick around and dominate. There is a long-established belief that a man has the right to do exactly what he likes in his own home. The police have always been highly reluctant to intervene in cases of domestic disputes, even where there is violence on the part of the man. If they do, it often happens that the wife is reluctant to give evidence in court against her abuser, particularly if there are children involved and her husband is the breadwinner.

The institution of marriage actually encourages the negative traits in men's personalities, and the pioneer Christians were aware of this all those centuries ago.

In early Christianity the only independent and autonomous women – those who were most certainly not afraid of men – were those who had forsaken marriage and children for the religious life. The choice of being immured in a nunnery or being immured in marriage may not strike the woman of today as a very attractive one, but for many centuries those were the only alternatives. Not every woman, or every man, had to get married. In fact, remaining single was considered the better, more Christian decision.

Once Protestantism took hold, celibacy and the monastic life became completely devalued and society changed drastically as a result. Although it is true that by the sixteenth century many convents and monasteries had become corrupt and their inmates were often lax, luxury-loving, selfish and base, the fact remains that an alternative to marriage and the family existed – an alternative which was swept away by the Reformation.

Religion, as the historian R.H. Tawney points out in his book *Religion and the Rise of Capitalism*, was largely responsible for the expansionist policies of the Tudors and Stuarts, and governments thereafter. After the Reformation, acquisition became the name of the game in all Protestant countries. The great Elizabethan explorers Sir Francis Drake, Sir Walter Raleigh and Sir Richard Grenville all began their exploits during the first flushes of Protestantism. With their predilections for plunder, empire-building, and converting the rest of the world – the 'dark-skinned unbelievers' – to their religion, Protestants encouraged the worst aspects of masculinity to develop and expand. Since the Reformation, the world has become more and more male-orientated, and one reason for this is that the world has so few valid, socially acceptable alternatives to marriage. There is even a move within the Catholic Church to allow priests to marry. Bachelorhood and spinsterhood are now seen as undesirable and odd, whereas formerly it was marriage that was considered second-rate.

In all societies where there is no real alternative to marriage, there is a huge discrepancy between the roles and expectations of men and women. In a society where being single is considered normal and entirely acceptable, there is no reason why both men and women should not achieve equally. In all-male monasteries men cook and sew without considering themselves effeminate for doing so. In all-female convents women garden, build, learn Latin and write learned works. Where there is no alternative to marriage, roles become polarized and those usually assigned to men acquire greater status.

Unholy Matrimony

In Islamic countries, where marriage is universally encouraged and expected and men may legally take four wives (no corresponding licence is granted to women), women count for virtually nothing. Masculine qualities are extolled at the expense of feminine virtues and women have no say in society and no power at any level. This goes a long way to explaining why the Middle East is always at war, and looks likely to be for some time yet. Wherever marriage is universal women have little influence and the worse excesses of (male) bad behaviour tend to run unchecked and unpunished. It is commonly said that women have absolute power in the home, but that power is fairly insignificant. Their 'reward' for giving up their independence for marriage is commonly seen as their opportunity to produce 'fine sons' for their husbands. Wherever marriage is elevated, sons instantly become more important than daughters.

Marriage encourages women to grow up dependent and men to grow up dominant and believing they are superior, just because of their sex.

In societies where marriage is the norm and nobody even thinks of avoiding it, there is also a huge difference in the way that men and women are educated. From the very first they are educated for their adult roles – their roles within marriage. In the Middle Ages, in Britain, when women were allowed autonomy, many of them became very learned (Julian of Norwich was a famous example). After the Reformation, it was considered that women did not need an education, as they were only going to get married and reproduce. Education, it was thought, was completely wasted on girls. Vestiges of that belief remain today and certainly in countries which encourage early marriage there is no equality of either education or opportunity. Women who have little choice but to marry are educated only in the domestic arts, in pleasing men and taking care of children. They are not allowed to play any part in the outside world. A tiny few rebel, but they are not generally admired for doing so – by either sex. The consequence of this is that children are brought up to imagine they are superior or inferior simply through the accident of gender. This is why, in the world at large, many men who lack both talent and ability can rise to high positions whereas clever, capable women are pushed at the earliest possible opportunity into marriage.

The concept of male superiority is encouraged by marriage and may at first sight seem a good thing, at least for men. But a little reflection soon reveals that the notion that maleness in itself confers superiority is a dangerous myth, leading to the power complex that ultimately causes wars.

So how does marriage, which is supposed to be a peaceable institution, a bastion of love and a safe haven for children, even a holy sacrament, become responsible for so many bad things? The answer is that if untalented, incapable or wrong-thinking men are allowed to shine simply because they are men, the idea that males are inherently superior will take hold, grow and allow them to commit evil and depraved acts without a trace of shame. From believing they are superior to women it is a very short step for men to decide they are also superior to certain other men. They believe they can tell other men, and hence whole societies, what to do. White men have commonly believed themselves superior to dark-skinned people, and it was this belief which allowed them to empire-build with such ferocity, to plunder Africa for slaves to work on sugar plantations and put the native population of India at their beck and call. Because these men had been brought up to believe that women were not of great value to the world, they found it quite easy to believe that other races, other species, did not matter much either.

Men who grow up in homes where the male is regarded as inherently superior find it quite easy to be cruel to animals. Today we have farming methods which turn the stomachs of all sensitive people – yet they continue, because there is a widespread belief that animals exist simply to serve us, as women exist simply to serve men. This same attitude also extends to the natural environment, which men arrogantly regard as something to be used and adapted as they like.

In the past people who spoke out against cruelty to animals or the despoiling of the natural landscape were regarded as sentimental and unrealistic. Farmers argue that their battery and broiler methods have ensured that all families can have eggs, chickens and turkeys every day instead of as an occasional treat. Intensive crop-rearing methods are justified on the grounds that everybody can now eat oranges and apples all the year round, instead of only when they are in season. The fact that the chickens and turkeys might have a miserable existence, reared in artificial conditions in order to satisfy human greed, is of no consequence to the farmers. As woman is made for man, so is the rest of creation. And now we are belatedly realizing that there is a huge price to pay for this plunder. As men demand their rights in marriage, so they demand that nature should give more than it reasonably can – and it never occurs to the majority of men that you have to give as well as take.

It may seem far-fetched to claim that there is a connection between such malpractices and the custom of near-compulsory marriage, but there is one. The family unit is the society in microcosm, so where men automatically take the upper hand in the home they will soon come to believe they have every right to take command in every outside situation. If in their youth they are encouraged to do exactly as they wish, without restraint, they will carry a high-handed attitude into their adult lives which could eventually prove dangerous and damaging.

The poet Shelley, an early feminist and hostile critic of the institution of marriage, recognized this. Marriage by his day had been formalized in a binding legal contract, unseverable except by Act of Parliament; severance – divorce – was available only to men who could pay £1000, and women were not allowed to petition for divorce.

Shelley, like so many men before and after him, failed to follow in practice what he advocated in theory. In theory he believed that women and men were equal, or could be so if untrammelled by marriage. In practice, he was married twice, both times to teenage girls who could not defend themselves and had no choice but to throw in their lot with him – however uncomfortable. Uncomfortable it was, as they both kept getting pregnant. Shelley's first wife, Harriet Westbrook, drowned herself in the Serpentine on learning that her husband had fallen in love with another woman, Mary Godwin (who, as Mary Shelley, became the author of *Frankenstein*). By the age of 24, when she became a widow, Mary had been pregnant five times and lost all but one of her children. The relentless succession of pregnancies undermined the health, character and confidence of both Mary and Harriet.

Shelley's mistake, in advocating free and equal unions between men and women, was to believe that physical sex was essential to them. He believed that through carnal contact one could attain some measure of the divine, achieve a spiritual communion. Many men have upheld this ideal, though with little justification. Shelley was not, however, personally promiscuous, nor was he in favour of sex without love, which was all too common within marriage.

In Shelley's day, equality of the sort he envisaged was impossible, because birth control methods were crude and largely ineffective and Shelley did not agree with Malthus' pronouncement that married chastity was the way to keep the population within limits. However, in our own time we have seen that even practically foolproof contraception has not equalized unions between men and women.

Shelley hated the idea of marital sexual fidelity and monogamy, as many poets and people of artistic temperament have, knowing that such unions enslave and entrap. He also understood that where there is inequality in marriage it leads to iniquitous inequalities in societies as a whole.

Shelley's feminist and socialist ideas are described in Paul Foot's book *Red Shelley*, in which the author disposes of the notion that Shelley was a dreamy romantic and puts him instead firmly in the category of revolutionary reformer. Shelley knew that the only real way to transform society was from the bottom, and we would do well to begin by abolishing legal marriage and replacing it with free and equal unions of whatever duration the partners wished.

In his most feminist poem, 'The Revolt of Islam', Shelley declares:

> Never will peace and human nature meet
> Till free and equal men and women greet

> Domestic peace; and ere this power can make
> In human hearts its calm and holy seat
> This slavery must be broken.

In the poem Shelley also asks: 'Can man be free if woman be a slave?', pointing out that half of humankind is in slavery, a prey to lust and hate. He saw that a society founded, as his was, on inequality, promoted a 'morality of suffering'.

The impetus for change, for the overthrow of marriage, had to come from women, he believed. As his society was ordered, men may have felt they had little to gain by freeing women, so it was up to women to lead the revolution. Women have never been very good at leading revolutions, though they often play an active part in them, and this may be why, whenever there is a revolution, things rapidly return to a close approximation of what they were before: there has never been any real input from the female side.

Women's oppression, in Shelley's view, meant the oppression of whole sections of humanity, of subject races and classes. Shelley did not want female domination, any more than he was in favour of male domination, but wanted a free and equal society untainted by corruption and bullying.

But women never became the leaders of a revolt against the status quo, and after Shelley's protests the sexes became even more unequal and polarized, in the Victorian era – the time of greatest expansion, greatest cruelty to 'subject races' and greatest female enslavement.

In seeing marriage as a union of slave and tyrant, Shelley was, as Paul Foot observes, reflecting the ideas of the French Revolution, which held that marriage should be abolished and children brought up in common, regardless of their parentage. Shelley's father-in-law, William Godwin, had written:

> It is absurd that the inclinations of two human beings should coincide through any long period of time. To oblige them to live and act together is to subject them to some inevitable portion of thwarting, bickering and unhappiness. Marriage is law and the worst of all laws, an affair of property and the worst of all properties.

Mary Wollstonecraft, who married Godwin, appealed to

women to summon up enough strength of mind and purpose to stop behaving to men as their 'toy and rattle'. Shelley took these ideas to heart and expanded them. In his view, the current doctrine of male superiority allowed a man to exploit and tyrannize not just the women in his home but everybody else – other human beings, other races, other nations. Men grew up believing they had a perfect right to bully those they considered to be beneath them, simply because they were given in the home power they did not deserve and had not earned.

Shelley believed that monogamous marriage was unnatural, and that it was not ordained by God, but simply a social convenience which had grown up to the disbenefit of both sexes, particularly women. He regarded legal marriage as little better than prostitution, because it was an arrangement in which love, being neither freely given nor freely received, could not possibly be kept alive. Most children, Shelley wrote, grow up in an atmosphere of squabbling and bickering, of power struggles, male domination and female acquiescence: 'They are nursed in a systematic school of ill-humour, violence and falsehood,' he claimed. So much for our fond belief that in previous centuries love and harmony reigned supreme within the domestic circle.

Shelley recognized that marriage forced women to be financially dependent on men as they were denied any income or profession of their own and could therefore never realize their full potential. He felt that the imposition of codes of conduct by legal means or religion served only to increase fear, jealousy and negativity in human relationships. In short, Shelley saw that marriage laws had exactly the opposite effect from what was intended – to encourage human beings to be more loving and caring to one another.

It has long been widely believed that without marriage laws men and women would descend rapidly into savagery, that men would take no responsibility for their children and that women would have no protection whatever in society. Marriage laws are supposed to exert a restraining influence on human sexual behaviour and to make those with responsibilities towards others discharge them. The Church's claim that marriage is a holy

Unholy Matrimony

ordinance has invested the vows taken to honour these obligations with the status of a sacrament.

These views still generally prevail, with occasional fluctuations. In the 1960s, for example, some men and a few misguided women advocated 'open marriage', or marriage without the 'piece of paper', but what that often meant in practice was the freedom for men to have as much sex as they wanted with as many different women as they pleased. Marilyn French, author of *Beyond Power: Men, Women and Morals*, observes that, in her country, the men are getting richer all the time and women poorer, because men so often desert their wives and families, without even paying maintenance if they can help it. They get married, get bored and run away, evading their responsibilities and leaving the abandoned women to look after the couple's offspring. As they do not have, or do not take, responsibility for children, they have more freedom to walk out and never come back. According to Marilyn French, men never have that same closeness and regard for their children that women have: the relationship is always more distant.

Also, many men pay lip-service to marriage while having affairs on the side – keeping mistresses, molesting young girls or boys, having homosexual liaisons . . . Men, one suspects, often marry more for show than for any other motive. Large numbers of them seem to find it impossible to be faithful in marriage; they would prefer several wives, or rather several women to attend to their needs without any of them getting jealous or possessive. It has long been assumed that women are the possessive, jealous sex and that men keep trying to wriggle out of being confined. As Byron said:

> Women are but the margin of our lives.
> The course flows on unheeded.

This arrogant attitude is something countless women have tried to alter, without conspicuous success. One of the reasons why marriage in its present form does not work is that men and women, as observed earlier in this book, have widely differing expectations of what the institution can provide. Basically, all the average man wants is somebody who will cook, clean, be a willing body in bed and, preferably, an attractive adornment at his elbow in public. As men go up the ladder of success they can, as is well known, attract prettier and more covetable women. Very few men regard women as individuals – they are blondes, brunettes, pairs of long legs, big breasts, or whatever, and are discussed in such terms, or rather cruder ones, in pubs and bars.

Marriages fail mostly because men and women are basically incompatible. Very few men bother to get to know women at all well, whereas women commonly monitor every little thing about their husbands, and try to emulate them and support them as much as possible. You could say this is the slave mentality coming out; but in fact there seems to be something in the female psyche that makes women simply more interested in people as individuals, more perceptive of their behaviour, more sensitive to their emotions, whereas most men tend to be interested only in themselves. Yet very few men are able, or willing, to analyse their own behaviour, or to think about what effect they might be having on other people. The one group of exceptions to this generalization is the artists, considerable numbers of whom have been of a homosexual inclination. It is a commonplace, however, that heterosexual men of an artistic and creative inclination commonly make the very worst husbands. The examples are legion: Dylan Thomas, Augustus John, Mozart, Arthur Koestler, Karl Marx, James Boswell. Many men who are high achievers have made life extremely unhappy for their wives and families. Marriage, rather than compounding happiness, as it is theoretically supposed to do, often serves to increase misery many times, cramping the style, perhaps, of the family's star performer and causing him to vent his anger and frustration on those to whom he is bound by convention.

Men are, as a sex, far more conventional than women; they are far more concerned about what others think about them and about what looks good, or right. Status symbols matter much more to men than they do to women, too. The average man is quite content as long as things seem all right on the surface. The selfish, self-centred ones are often immune to what is really happening within their personal relationships. So long as they can get married, so long as they can keep a wife who stays more or less in her place, so long as they have a decent home, a job, a car and a reasonable standard of living, they can muddle along. A majority of men would probably agree with Joe Lampton in John Braine's novel *Room at the Top* who declares, memorably: 'It's not what I want, it's what I'll settle for.' Men often seem far more tolerant of a bad situation than women do. This could be because, even today, men have more outlets than women in marriage, and more escape routes from boredom or friction. They are less tied to the home, partly because of their jobs but even more because their emotional commitment is likely to be far weaker than that of their wives. They tend not to feel guilty and anxious in the same way or to the same degree as women, and have an enviable ability to pretend nasty things are not happening.

Men tend to be more hypocritical and devious than women, and to indulge in wishful thinking, which can make it hard to believe that many of them too are beginning to realize how much of modern marriage is a nonsense. Although some of them may proclaim, from the pulpit and in Parliament, that God intended us to be monogamous, married and heterosexual, and may advocate a return to the imagined 'traditional values', many of those who proclaim the loudest are those who are having affairs on the side, whose own marriages have broken up, or who have had homosexual liaisons. Those people aside, many more realistic men are turning their backs on marriage – on the very institution which was ordained for men by men and for the enhancement of men's lives. I recently met a large group of gay teachers and lecturers, and asked them why they thought homosexuality was so much on the increase. They had no hesitation in replying that the main reason was because heterosexual relationships had become so bad, such a power struggle, so full of hostility and resentment, that many were now preferring the more equal and honest relationships they were able to have with members of their own sex.

There was not the same possessiveness, they said, with a male lover. Men do not want to own other men as women commonly do and, of course, there is blessed total freedom from the possibility of children. The gay men I spoke to reckoned that they could have far better relationships with members of their own sex. Lesbians have said the same thing. If heterosexual marriage really *were* divinely ordained, as we are told, gay and lesbian relationships would not proliferate as they do. Often people who have been in both heterosexual and homosexual relationships say they far prefer the latter, simply because somebody of the same sex is more likely to understand them.

The claustrophobic togetherness now seen as compulsory in modern marriage is itself driving people into alternative kinds of relationships. Men, even heterosexual ones, certainly do not like being with their wives all the time – they never have – and wives do not really enjoy relying solely on their husbands for company. But they know this is what society expects, and thus married people are becoming more miserable than ever.

It is perhaps as well that men are starting to turn their backs on marriage, for in the very near future there simply will not be enough women to go round. In the past, owing to the frequency of wars and the greater physical weakness of male babies, there was always a surplus of women. However, by 1993, according to the predictions of the Family Policy Studies Centre, there will be many more males of marriageable age than females. This in itself could mean that men come to have a different outlook on marriage. If women are statistically rarer, they will have more power in relationships. The statistician Kathleen Kiernan, of the Centre for Economic Policy Research, London, predicts that the coming surplus of men will profoundly affect marriage, and will mean that there will in future be far more unions based on mutual consent without legal bonds. Women, she says, will no longer feel the need to grab their man as soon as possible, in case they miss out, as they will be freed by their new sense of 'rarity'. She also says that families of the future will be smaller than ever, and childbirth will be delayed, as women no longer rush into marriage for fear of being left 'on the shelf'.

It is the men who will be the old maids of the future. This, according to the statisticians, will be a potent factor in changing their attitudes towards marriage. Women will be able to be, as men have always been, cavalier and uncaring. No longer is there an economic necessity on the part of women to get married as soon as possible, nor need there be any worry about getting pregnant. Most people who study and interpret population statistics feel that there are profound changes to come in attitudes towards marriage and children which have as yet hardly begun.

New situations are forcing new attitudes. As yet, most of us are living in the past, and seeing marriage as it used to be, rather than as it is, or as it could be. We have hardly considered the possibility of completely different kinds of relationships, based not on property and ownership but on friendship and freedom. Such relationships are now entirely possible, yet very few people have as yet realized this. We have been brought up in such a strong tradition of men and women owning each other that we can hardly imagine any other way to relate. Now that women are becoming statistically rarer, attitudes must change.

Another factor, almost perversely, is forcing a change – on behalf of men. In spite of the power invested in married men by law, many husbands feel they are dominated and henpecked by their wives. A Mr Patrick Ridley, of Romford, Essex, recently started a Henpecked Husbands Society, and claimed in a newspaper interview: 'We are becoming a nation of frightened ninnies in pinnies.' Women, he complained, were now telling men what to do, how to behave, how to conduct their lives. He claimed that although his society had started out as a joke, he had discovered a real human need. Indeed, stories of henpecked husbands frequently emerge in court cases. One husband endured 35 years during which he was never allowed his own cheque book and was sometimes made to sleep in the car.

Some men find it difficult to believe that husbands could allow themselves to be henpecked, and wonder how they, the supposedly stronger and more powerful partners, could have put up with it. The truth is that any man, even the most domineering one, can be henpecked, once the woman has been able to call his bluff. Many get away with appalling behaviour, simply because their partners have become cowed and frightened. Once people get like this they are living only half-lives; unfortunately, the institution of marriage encourages such vices.

Ideally, we should be able to live with other people in peace and harmony, each enhancing the other's lives. What often happens instead is that one partner becomes dominant at the expense of the other. The dominant one continues to dominate through fear of the other getting the upper hand. Such is the result of the romance, love and togetherness we fondly envisage when we walk up the aisle.

Even outwardly strong men find that they can collapse when the reality of their marriage comes home to them. American research carried out at the Family Psychicenter in St Louis, Missouri, has revealed that men can easily disintegrate when under severe emotional pressure at home. The researchers analysed the psychiatric backgrounds of sixteen prominent men, presidents of major corporations, successful lawyers, politicians and doctors. They found that underneath their aura of confidence and success these men were childlike, 'expressing profound feelings of helplessness, desperation, inadequacy and confusion'. In marriage they had tried to force their wives into a submissive, dependent type of relationship, so that they could be the boss at home as well as at work. When the wives eventually tired of their husbands' behaviour and started to assert themselves, the worlds of these ostensibly powerful men collapsed. Their relationships were revealed as having been built on sand.

In all marital relationships built on power/dominance on the one side and submission/dependence on the other, there is bound to be a time of reckoning. Both partners are acting wrongly and in due course a price will have to be paid, either in unending hostility or in the collapse of the marriage.

In modern marriage the blind lead the blind. Women, having been fed a diet of romance, believe that their men will be strong, protective and loving – even if they exhibit no such characteristics before marriage. Many brides assume that marriage will change their chosen partner for the better. Men enter marriage believing that they are going to be looked after, admired and given pleasure by their wives, whom they expect to be attractive, ever-willing in bed, providing endless hot, nourishing meals, a clean home, clean shirts and children who will be a credit to him. These concepts of married life are a fantasy, for both sexes, and are soon revealed as such.

Although all the studies show that men's health tends to be better within marriage, and that marriage benefits men far more than it does women, many men find that once they get used to living alone they vastly prefer it. Artistic and literary men, particularly, have often found that they can work better and be more creative on their own. The novelist Simon Raven, a bachelor for many years, once said on a radio programme: 'Women can be such a frightful bloody nuisance. They are possessive, jealous, illogical, even when intelligent, and boringly domestic. And they will breed all the time.'

The cartoonist Frank Dickens, creator of Bristow, also prefers to live alone. He was married to a Spanish woman for fourteen years, and has said of their relationship: 'When we met, she spoke no English and I didn't speak a word of Spanish. When she learned to speak English, she found she didn't like me.'

An idea has always prevailed that bachelors are lucky, because they have escaped the snares of scheming women. The reality is in fact the other way round: women who manage to escape matrimony are the lucky ones, for they can remain individuals, answerable only to themselves, all their lives. Men who remain single are theoretically the unlucky ones, as statistics show that they are likely to have worse health and inferior jobs, and will tend to die earlier than married men. But the problem is that large numbers of men, like women, marry for completely the wrong reasons – because they fear being lonely, because they want guaranteed sex, because they want to have power over somebody in their lives, because they want, or need, an heir, or because to be single for too long looks odd, unless you declare yourself to be gay.

The journalist Martin Plimmer recently observed in *The Sunday Times*: 'All bachelors have watched married friends turn into dullards or decline into internecine bitterness.' One bachelor quoted by Plimmer said: 'I think married men are unhappy in a different way. If a horse had the same chance of success in a race, I wouldn't back it. I know only five happy couples.'

If women are almost universally unhappy in marriage, then men will be too. In such close daily contact, it is impossible for one person to be happy if the other is miserable. Misery, like happiness, spreads and is infectious, and misery in marriage is all too common, simply because the two partners are too tightly bound to one another by emotion and convention. It is not always realized that you can be deeply attached negatively as well as positively.

Both women and men have much to gain by the abolition of formalized marriage – and very little, if anything, to lose.

7

Marriage, money and the law

You do not have to be a radical feminist to realize that marriage, by its very nature, creates sexual inequality. When the present marriage laws were encoded by Lord Hardwicke in 1753, he set up a monument to female dependency. Now, though we have made some strides towards greater financial and legal independence for women, the notion of submission and dependence is still endemic within marriage.

British politicians are currently attempting to make taxation laws fairer to married people, and married women in particular. While recognizing that there are many anomalies, politicians are yet trying to 'honour' the institution of marriage, so that married people are no longer penalized for committing themselves to one another. As the taxation and social security laws operate at present, single men and single women are treated as equals in matters of finance (unless there is 'cohabitation', which will be discussed later). When a man and a woman say 'I do', however, the situation alters fundamentally. Henceforth, a woman's income, earned and unearned, is added to her husband's, unless she opts for separate taxation, which is not financially beneficial unless the couple have a joint taxable income of over £27,000 (in 1988). As such couples are in the minority, separate taxation is rarely applied.

This is all about to change. Vociferous demands by women's groups have at last encouraged the Conservative government to alter the rules so that married women will have more privacy and independence where money is concerned. In 1990 the notion that a married woman's income belongs to her husband will be swept away, and both partners will be taxed separately on both earned and unearned income. This is a long overdue reform and an entirely logical one. But the proposals *still* greatly differentiate between the married and the unmarried state. For instance, although all married couples in which both partners earn are to be taxed separately, they will receive an extra allowance for being a married couple as well as their individual allowances.

For many years, British politicians have been concerned that taxation and social security laws favour the unmarried. They have felt that it is wrong for people to be penalized for getting married rather than 'living in sin'. But equal taxation in the context of the present marriage laws is an impossibility. If marriage alters a person's status in law, it will of necessity alter his or her taxable position. In law one is either a separate individual or one is not. You can't have it both ways. If marriage were abolished as an institution, men and women would have to be treated as equals.

In some ways, the new proposals are a backward step, as they try to encourage people to get married rather than simply living together. Until August 1988 two unmarried people – of either opposite sexes or the same sex – buying a house could each claim tax relief on the mortgage. A married couple were a 'unit' whereas an unmarried couple were regarded as two separate individuals. This anomaly has now been removed and tax relief on mortgage interest payments is tied to the mortgaged property rather than the tax-paying purchaser. The intention is to treat married and unmarried couples identically, and thus remove the incentive (of double tax relief) to 'live in sin'. The legislation has simultaneously promoted the cause of marriage and increased the amount of revenue due to the state. But as financial journalist Sarah Hogg pointed out in an article in *The Independent* in March 1988:

Since the married state has happily survived even a hostile tax climate, there is little evidence that people need to be bribed to keep it alive.

Nobody today would argue, I think, with the notion that married women and men should be taxed separately, on both earned and unearned income. The real question lies in why anybody should, these days, want to keep the state institution of marriage 'alive'.

The tax plans, which come into effect in 1990, do not by any means remove all differences between married and unmarried people. The new 'married couple's' allowance will be worth the same as the former married man's supplement, and the proposal is that it will be paid to the husband, as before – if he has enough income to benefit. Otherwise, it will go to the wife.

Although the tax reforms will give financial independence to career women, they will not of course make any difference at all to the status of the non-earning wife who is financially dependent on her husband. Women who do not earn will be no better off than before. Patricia Hewitt, an executive of the Labour Party, says: 'Being married and a man will go on attracting a valuable prize from the Inland Revenue.' The worst aspect of the new plans, perhaps, is that although the married man's allowance is to be abolished, the new married couple's allowance will continue to be paid *to the man*. A married man earning exactly the same as his wife will therefore be about £7 a week better off than she is, or than a single man would be: not a lot of money, perhaps, but it makes a symbolic difference.

Surely the only way to be completely fair is to end the current change of status on marriage and make all men and women legally single and financially independent of each other.

'How so?' you may ask. What would actually happen in practice? What about women who prefer not to work, so that they can bring up children? Will it not mean that all mothers will be living on state benefit, eking out a poverty-stricken existence while men get richer and richer? Surely the whole purpose of marriage laws is the protection of women and children? Perhaps; but the other side of protection is submission. If someone is considered to be in need of protection, this means he or she is automatically assumed to be in a weak position. Women are placed in a position of weakness and dependence by the very existence of the marriage laws.

In their book *Cohabitation Without Marriage* academic lawyers

Unholy Matrimony

Michael D.A. Freedman and Christina M. Lyon argue this case strongly, and reveal that cohabitation laws are growing up alongside marriage laws which are becoming almost as restrictive. As there is no current statutory definition of cohabitation, they have defined it for the purposes of their book as a 'non-legalized pair-bond relationship'. Even though marriage in its present form is only two-and-a-half centuries old, we have grown up with the idea that it is sacred and unalterable. This has led lawyers to formulate cohabitation laws that approximate as closely as possible to those of marriage, to try to continue the notion of female dependency.

What Freedman and Lyon call the 'cereal packet' norm of father going out to work, happy housewife mother and a couple of kids is actually a very late creation in the history of humankind. It grew up with capitalism: as the workplace was increasingly separated from the home and men went out to work, so women's work became restricted to the household; the man wanted his home to be above all a haven where he could be looked after and withdraw from the problems of the world. Thus the family took its modern form and the cult of domesticity grew and grew until it reached its present proportions.

Freedman and Lyon consider that the oppression of women lies in the privatized family of today, and that the tax and legal situation merely intensifies and underlines this oppression. Within the family, women are expected to be dependent on men, and even if they are not the law still treats them as if they are. The notion that a man is head of the household will remain enshrined in the new British tax laws because *he* will be paid the married couple's allowance.

The American feminist Kate Millett once said: 'As long as woman's place is defined as separate, a male-dominated society will define her place as inferior.' That inferiority is part and parcel of, and indissoluble from, the marriage laws. The continued existence of the married man's allowance (under another name) preserves privilege for the male, and means that the woman's wage is still seen as supplementary, not the significant breadwinning one. The present law, say Freedman and Lyon, claims many justifications for treating men and women differently in law. Yet, they maintain, it is the law itself which makes women inferior in marriage and financial matters. Women they write, cannot be at one and the same time married as we understand marriage, and independent.

Though the foregoing discussion relates only to British law, a little research will reveal that in *all* countries married women are treated differently from single women. In some more 'advanced' countries, particularly Scandinavia, cohabitation laws have become more fully codified, but where this has happened men and women are *still* treated differently once they decide to live together.

As for fiscal policies, married women in Britain are still largely excluded from social security benefit. Supplementary benefit (now called 'income support'), sickness and unemployment benefits, pensions and family income supplement are all based on the premise that a woman is dependent on a man. A married woman continues to be dependent, as the law sees it, even if her husband (or cohabitee) is not earning any money but is himself dependent upon state handouts. When a woman does not have a male protector, she is penalized even more. For though we feel sorry for widows, and try to 'make it up to' them, few people feel sorry for unmarried mothers. These people are still castigated by society, albeit less than was once the case.

When the welfare state was set up in the late 1940s, William Beveridge, the architect of the plan, decided to regard a married couple as a 'team' rather than as independently-functioning individuals. The social security system still embodies this notion, even though society has changed greatly in the past forty or so years. The sexual relationship, it seems, is the significant factor, and if a man and a woman are living 'as husband and wife', the woman is assumed in law to be dependent on the man.

The so-called 'cohabitation rule' which has angered so many women seeks to establish whether a woman is in fact living with a man are a continuing sexual relationship. If she is, her own benefits may be curtailed. Freedman and Lyon say, *à propos* of this, that if the cohabitation rule were removed it would reveal the inequality and dependence inherent in marriage. The continuing assumption is that if a man is living with a woman, he is supporting her.

The family income supplement, introduced in the 1970s, is an added cash benefit a man may receive when he is in full-time work but his earnings are deemed to be below the current poverty level. A married woman may not claim this benefit, and in a family in which the man stays at home and the woman works, similarly, she is not able to claim. Where a couple are living together 'as man and wife', again, only the man can claim. A woman is allowed to claim this supplement only if she is bringing up a child alone and there is no man in sight.

It is also assumed that a woman looks after a man at home, and that this is in fact her job. Allowances are claimable by men when their wives are incapacitated and unable to do their household duties: the reverse does not apply.

Family law, as Freedman and Lyon explain, is limited to a 'narrow conceptualization of monogamous marriage and the nuclear family as the only models for intimacy'. The present divorce laws also make the assumption that a woman is financially dependent upon a man. He is usually the one who pays maintenance after the marriage has ended, not only to the children (as of course he should) but also to his ex-wife, who can keep taking him to court to get her maintenance payments increased.

As marriage is no longer, in the West at least, primarily a property exchange or a dynastic arrangement, it might be wondered what it has to recommend it, and why so many people should be determined to uphold, protect and preserve the institution. In all probability the reasons are mainly sentimental and adhered to out of habit: no evidence exists to show that the married state is in any way preferable to remaining single in law.

In some countries it is now rapidly becoming the norm to live together without marrying, and financial legislation is reflecting this. In Sweden, for example, social security arrangements now actively discourage marriage, and all over Scandinavia people are voting with their feet and deciding to live together without getting married. There is no evidence whatever that these more informal unions are more liable to break up, that children are treated worse, or that women are placed in an even weaker position than is the case with formal marriages.

One of the anomalies of the present system is that we don't know what we are committing ourselves to when we marry. None of us makes contracts in Britain at the moment, and no lawyer is present when a couple gets married. Although marriage contracts are now common in certain states of America, in British law they have no binding force. We simply acquiesce to an automatic alteration of status.

Freedman and Lyon observe: 'The state-imposed marriage contract assumes a limited, sex-based, traditional family form; the union of a single man and woman who commit themselves to each other.'

Their view is that the present marriage patterns are simply relics of a bygone age, no longer relevant, and they argue that, instead of marriage laws which treat everybody the same, laws of cohabitation should be established that make provision for individual needs. Thus, a couple would be able to work out their own terms of living together, or cohabiting, and could have them ratified by a lawyer. This would mean that marriage would once more become a business arrangement, a partnership set up to suit the individual partners, and which could be dissolved or altered as circumstances changed.

It is often argued that if state marriage laws were to disappear the whole of society would resort to anarchy. This is why politicians are now pressing for tax reforms which would perpetuate the differences between those who are married and those who simply live together. What they want is to take away the financial advantages that have for so long attached to living with another person while remaining unmarried.

The controversial 'poll tax', or rather community charge, which is to replace rates, will certainly treat married couples as a unit. Husbands and wives will be responsible for each other's tax. This is anomalous, because in no other situation are husbands and wives any longer responsible for each other's debts.

Whether greater financial independence will make any difference to the numbers of people getting married, the length of time marriages last or the level of personal happiness the participants enjoy remains to be seen. It seems unlikely.

I would like to see all people treated as single for the whole of their lives, whether they cohabit or not, whether they have children or not. This would mean that men and women would be equally able to claim the appropriate state benefits, provided they were entitled to them. Women who did not choose to work because they had young children would not be obliged to work, but would be in exactly the same *legal* position as unemployed men. This would not necessarily mean that they would have only state benefits to rely on.

If a couple decided to live together, they could draw up a legal contract to suit both of them; this could ensure that the man paid maintenance and took responsibility for any children that resulted from the union.

Any distinctions between legitimate and illegitimate children would vanish, and all would be equally able to inherit. In fact, this has more or less happened in law already, and is yet another argument for the abolition of marriage. Absence of marriage ties would mean that people would be able to leave their money where they wanted, to a cats' home if that was their wish, and nobody would be entitled, or feel they were entitled, to claim the money. At the moment, it is possible for a person to leave money to a spouse without the bequest being liable to inheritance tax, but not to anybody else. Moreover, a marital partner may not be turned out of the marital home on death. All these points of law simply underline one principle: that men and women who marry thereafter have a claim on each other's money and property.

Under my proposals, all women with children who were not economically active would be able to take advantage of the money which would be available to them by abolition of the married man's, or rather married couple's, tax allowance. If marriage were abolished, all the anomalies currently relating to husbands' and wives' incomes would also go.

Child benefit, which currently amounts to about £7.25 a week per child, is claimed by many women with young children to be their only bit of 'independence', especially if this is their sole source of income apart from what their husbands allow them for housekeeping. If marriage were abolished, child benefit could be replaced by proper state benefits which a woman with children could receive on her own behalf if she were not working.

It could be argued that this proposed system would create an even greater discrepancy between rich and poor. But there are enormous discrepancies in the current system: some women are multi-millionaires, either by their own efforts, or by being left fortunes, or by marrying into them, while other women have to rely entirely on state benefits. Though my system could not eradicate such differences, it would do away entirely with the notion that a woman, especially if she has children, must be dependent upon a man.

In her book *Intimate Strangers* Lilian Rubin observes that for men independence is regarded as totally admirable, whereas for women it is generally something to fear. One of the reasons why women fear independence is that the whole thrust of society's laws is against female autonomy. Rubin goes on to say that most women she spoke to while researching the book had negative associations with the word independence, whereas only one man did. Women worry about being alone, about not being loved, protected, nurtured.

Women fear this, I believe, only because the attitude is encoded in our laws. As Freedman and Lyon say, if the law were changed, then what we imagine to be fundamental attitudes would also change.

Lilian Rubin also points out:

In an economy that is almost always short on jobs, and in which most men who are lucky enough to have one simply can't earn enough to meet the idealized notions of male responsibility, making it in the world of work is no less problematic than women subjugating themselves – especially when his successes are supposed to serve for hers as well. The disappointment of his own dreams would be hard enough to bear, but it hurts even more when a man must face the knowledge that he has dashed hers as well.

Unholy Matrimony

In a society based on the 'free and equal unions' which Shelley favoured so much (although it must not be forgotten that Shelley never actually earned his own living, and never explained how the financial affairs of such unions would be arranged), female subjugation and the disappointment which so often follows when a man does not turn out to be a good breadwinner would disappear, because people would grow up from birth knowing that they had to depend upon themselves.

I used to laugh at the Wages for Housework campaign, wondering why anybody should pay me to do my own housework (something I hated, was no good at, and certainly would not want paying for). Now that I have come to the conclusion that abolition of formal marriage would do only good, I see the campaign in a completely different light. The premise of wages for housework is that it would end, once and for all, female dependence on a male wage, as women would be paid for their services in running homes and bringing up children. A bulletin from the King's Cross Women's Centre, which runs the International Wages for Housework Campaign, stated that all women's work, waged and currently unwaged, should count economically. The Campaign argues that money presently spent, or 'wasted', on nuclear weapons should be diverted to paying women for the largely disregarded work they do in the house: looking after children, shopping, cleaning, cooking meals and often caring for elderly dependants as well. The Campaign's argument is that the world would stop running if women stopped doing this essential work, which at the moment is seen as part of their obligation to those who share their lives. Women, who often work hard and long hours, still have to depend on unregulated handouts from the men with whom they live. Paying women a wage for housework would end their present dependence, in some cases almost total, on men.

In an article on the so-called 'Poor Carolines' in the *Daily Telegraph* Alexandra Artley revealed that some wives whose husbands are earning £40,000 a year and more have to ask them for the price of a pair of tights. Society assumes, erroneously, that if a woman is married to a high-earning husband, she is also 'rich'. In fact, as Artley points out, many women in this position have simply no money of their own, and no means of getting any. Their weekly child benefit is their only independent income.

Our society has embraced the idea that what is his is also hers. Unfortunately, this does not always apply in practice, and many men use their financial advantage in other ways. The only way to end female dependence on men is to have a radical rethink about marriage. While we persist in the idea of coupledom and believe that a man should always support a woman, rather than the woman being able to support herself, we shall never gain equality.

As I see it, under the new regime a woman would either earn her own money, or she would receive state benefits of a reasonable order if she were unwilling or unable to find work, or looking after children. And she would be treated exactly like a single person, as single mothers are, in law. Of course, this does not mean that all women would immediately have to depend only on state handouts. Many would choose to work and be financially independent. If the understanding that women could not depend on men disappeared, women would find the strength to be more self-sufficient, to develop the sisterhood idea which, to date, has remained only a dream in the minds and hearts of a few. If women grew up with the idea that they have to be financially and emotionally independent, they would bring more pressure to bear for the establishment of more nurseries and crèches and for better wages. For despite the Equal Pay Act and its like, women do not earn equal pay for equal work; one of the factors that continues to militate against this is the deeply entrenched notion that a woman must depend upon a man, and that any wage she may earn is supplementary, rather than the one that matters. In many cases, of course, it *is* the lower wage, because much of the work traditionally done by women (nursing is a prime example) is severely undervalued and therefore low-paid.

While men are assumed to be major breadwinners and women grow up accepting this, women's wages will stay low, female part-timers will continue to be denied proper conditions and married women will be denied individual state benefits. Unfairness is at the very heart of marriage, and will continue to be so until marriage ceases to be part of the state system.

Unholy Matrimony

Even Barbara Cartland, in many ways the champion of men, is in favour of paying stay-at-home women a state wage to end their dependence on men. Perhaps she also recognizes that financial dependence encourages many negative personality traits to display themselves – in both sides of the partnership – and that few positive characteristics can come from a position of weakness and dependence.

Yet while governments persist in the cosy-couple concept of marriage and continue to invest marriage with sentimentality and religious significance, increasing numbers of people, all over the Western world, are deciding to live together without benefit of marriage. Freedman and Lyon cite examples from several countries: one in eight couples in Denmark and Sweden, they report, is now cohabiting rather than getting married; France has seen a rapid rise in cohabitation, with about half the couples who eventually marry formally cohabiting first; in the USA more than two million couples who have no intention of getting married are cohabiting; in Norway, Finland and Germany the cohabitation rate is about 15 per cent of all couples. Cohabitation is generally more common in Scandinavia than in other European countries.

What is happening now, in many Western countries, is that cohabitation laws are growing up alongside marriage laws, which is creating enormous confusion. As Freedman and Lyon see it, cohabitation laws are increasingly tending to imitate those governing marriage; soon there may be little difference, and the idea of female dependence could easily be enshrined in cohabitation laws as it has always been in marriage.

The reason that cohabitation laws are aping those of marriage is because society retains the idea that marriage is the norm. We now have, in many European countries and also in the USA, the peculiar situation of two sets of laws governing the basis on which two people should live together. As more and more people opt for cohabitation and decide to do away with the 'piece of paper', governments are creating legislation to make these liaisons as much like state marriage as possible.

This is a trend that Freedman and Lyon deplore, but which is probably inevitable while we persist in regarding marriage as 'the norm'. They also make the telling point that, however romantic and 'in love' one may be at the beginning of a relationship, in the final analysis human emotions usually run deepest where financial and property arrangements are concerned.

These are what the cohabitation laws are most concerned to protect – and now, not surprisingly, the language of economic dependence, which has characterized marriage for centuries, is starting to be heard in cohabitation laws. If one partner dies, the cohabitant may be provided for from the deceased person's estate. As the law now stands, a woman who has cohabited with a man and borne his child would have to prove, on his death, that she was dependent on him in order to gain access to his property, unless he had named her as beneficiary in a will. Making a will can, of course, overcome this problem. In default, however, dependence has to be proved in order that the surviving partner can benefit.

As the cohabitation laws stand at present, where there are children either party may apply to the courts for financial provision if the other person has failed to provide reasonable maintenance. The father is seen as having a duty to provide for his children, whether they are legitimately conceived or not. The law also states that if a woman has sacrificed her career to bring up children she should be entitled to maintenance, whether or not she is married. But although it is right that men should be made to provide for their offspring there is no excuse for laws passed in the 1980s to encourage the financial dependence of one sex upon the other.

Where cohabitation laws differ widely at present from those relating to married couples is in respect of criminal activities. In law, no spouse may ever be compelled to give evidence against the marriage partner, but a cohabitant may be so compelled. A husband may not currently be charged with raping his wife: a cohabitee may. A married person has some rights to the matrimonial home, even when there are no legal or equitable interests. A cohabitee has no such rights automatically, though it might well be that a cohabiting mother with offspring would have a strong claim in a court of law.

Otherwise, however, the differences between marriage and cohabitation are being eroded all the time, and the same narrowly defined family models are being applied to cohabitation – as if the nuclear, monogamous family were the only way to live and to relate to others.

In the USA, cohabitation is increasingly being treated as a shadow institution of marriage and is already ominously similar to the legal variety.

In Australia, too, the Family Relationship Act of 1975 entitles parties in a non-marital relationship to the same rights and benefits as legal spouses. Five years' continuous cohabitation is required for enforcement of this law. In Canada, cohabiting couples may now enter into contracts exactly as married people do; such contracts must be made in writing and witnessed to be legally binding. This idea could well be adopted in other countries.

The general trend in all countries formulating cohabitation laws is to treat marriage as the ideal and to approximate cohabitation laws to those of marriage as far as possible. But only cohabiting couples who are heterosexual and living in marriage-like relationships are covered by the legislation. A gay or lesbian relationship would not, in law, be categorized as cohabitation. The law recognizes only family-like relationships, marriage being seen as the proper basis for family life, and continues to regard women as economically dependent on men, whether they are or not.

In the past cohabitation was treated almost as a form of prostitution, and is still referred to, though now generally with tongue in cheek, as 'living in sin'. The sheer number of people who decide to live together without marriage has largely destroyed this perception, but cohabitation is increasingly regarded as virtually identical to marriage. It seems that there is no escape. Laws passed to protect the 'weak' work to make them submissive. Cohabitation laws have by no means been a step forward for feminism.

Freedman and Lyon, the authors of *Cohabitation Without Marriage*, end their book with the following comment:

In reality, the assimilation of cohabitation to marriage is a way of controlling women, a form of moral regulation. It would be better, we think, if marriage were to become more like cohabitation. The future lies with contract rather than with status, autonomy instead of supposed protection.

Women and men who wish to cohabit rather than marry may find themselves encumbered with all sorts of laws which they did not know about. The four co-authors of *The Cohabitation Handbook* observe that while current cohabitation laws reflect the rights and duties of marriage, the practice retains vestiges of a sinful relationship, which until recently all cohabitation was considered to be, therefore those living together 'as man and wife' may find their benefits cut because the woman is assumed to be under the 'protection' of a man, the supposedly stronger and higher-earning partner. Only one member of the partnership may claim social security, for example. This drawback does not apply in the case of lesbian and gay couples living together. It seems that it is the heterosexual couple which causes problems, because living together as a married couple without actually *being* married constitutes an anomaly in the eyes of the law. Hence the confusing situation *vis-à-vis* tax and benefits.

Any system, say the authors of *The Cohabitation Handbook,* which assumes female dependence upon a man is degrading to women. They argue, as I do, for individual and legally binding contracts instead of marriage. They claim that the advantage of a contract over state marriage is that the contract is a private agreement formulated in the interests of particular individuals, whereas marriage is a public matter as well as being a contract which is virtually impossible to end. Anybody who imagines that divorce ends a marriage, or legal obligations to the former partner, is sadly deceived. A contract, by contrast, can be brought to an end by mutual consent, and without the hostility and adversarial flavour which divorce seems to make almost inevitable The very word 'divorce' has negative connotations, whereas the formal ending of a business agreement implies not that the arrangement has failed, simply that it has come to the end of its useful life.

Pensions, too, lend credence to the idea that within marriage the woman is dependent upon the man. Occupational pension schemes usually make automatic provision for a widow's pension but not a widower's pension. This applies even when a woman in employment is paying exactly the same pension contributions as a man. A few years ago a woman surgeon employed at a top teaching hospital, where contribution to the pension scheme was compulsory, discovered that although the pensions of male surgeons in her position provided for dependants in case of death, hers did not. She found that in order to get the same level of benefit she would have to pay into two schemes. One reason why such unfairness continues is because pensions were expressly excluded from the Sex Discrimination Act. Another, undoubtedly, is because few people bother to read the small print, and the majority have very little idea as to what their pension will provide. The obfuscation might be partly deliberate, of course. How many people who have contributed to a company pension scheme, compulsory or not, have ever had it explained to them so that they know what benefits they and their dependants would get from it?

Pension schemes were originally designed to meet the needs of full-time male workers and have never been adapted to meet female workers' requirements. Their terms reflect the continuing assumption that women are financially dependent on their husbands, rather than the other way round. In order for a widower to claim his late wife's pension – as a woman would automatically claim her late husband's – he would have to demonstrate physical and mental incapacity. Such a situation is, of course, highly humiliating and degrading. Either pension schemes make provision for dependants or they do not. Moreover pension schemes usually make automatic provision for children in the case of male contributors whereas they do not for women.

Pension schemes also currently exclude part-time workers, most of whom are women. An Equal Opportunities survey carried out in January 1985 found that 96 per cent of pension schemes automatically provided a pension for the widow of a male member, whereas only 31 per cent provided a similar pension for a widower. Over 50 per cent of schemes made automatic provision for children of male members, yet only 28 per cent provided the same benefits for children of female members. These figures refer to schemes to which men and women contribute an equal amount of money and where employees have no choice to opt out of the scheme.

Hence the question arises as to whether a man or a woman *should* join a pension scheme which provides for his or her spouse. Should not that individual be independent? I myself do not believe in these schemes and would never by choice contribute to one where I had to pay in money now so that my husband could benefit on my death. Nor do I support the premise that a man should pay money in order to entitle his widow to a pension. All this merely lends weight to the idea that people have a duty to provide for their partners – people with whom they have decided to live not, nowadays, for financial reasons, but because they like them. We should be doing all we can to encourage strengths, not weaknesses, and financial independence rather than dependence.

I have seen many, many women change out of all recognition when they at last have some money of their own: not the pathetic sums involved in child benefit, but real money, which may come from earnings or from an inheritance. Older women, people who have never earned any money in their lives, suddenly come alive when they have money of their own. They become different people, more assertive, more independent in mind, more lively – even more intelligent. It seems as though some part of their personality has been permanently cut off by their never having had money of their own.

It is noticeable that when men become unemployed and financially dependent on their wives, their personalities often undergo a change for the worse and they become like the worst sort of dependent women – fearful, wheedling, manipulative, lacking in self-confidence and self-esteem. It is my belief that, in order to fulfil their potential as human beings, all adults need financial independence. Money should not affect personal relationships. It is much easier to love a person properly if you are not financially dependent upon him or her, and if each has a personal, private income which may be shared but which does not by right partially or wholly belong to the other person. In such a situation unions really can be 'free and equal', as in Shelley's phrase.

It is said that more marriages founder upon money problems than upon any other single factor. Those who divorce most easily nowadays are the less well-off, unpropertied classes, because they have least to lose by so doing. They will always get, as the bottom line, state benefits which will enable them to survive. For property owners, the decision to divorce is far more complicated. You literally do have more to lose when money is at stake. Yet in theory we no longer marry people *for* their money, but for the increased happiness we suppose a union will mutually bring about. If dependence and obligation to maintain were not built into heterosexual relationships so extensively we could all be more loving and giving, naturally. It may seem incredible that any woman could put herself in the position of having to ask for money for a pair of tights, but, as things stand, if you give up your independent career to bring up a family, or to follow your husband round the world in accordance with the requirements of his job, that is what happens. Married women are destined to be poverty-stricken, with no right to any money at all other than the paltry child benefit, or 'family credit' as it will be known in future. With the abolition of marriage, such dependence would vanish, and both sexes would be a lot better for it.

8

So what about the children?

Whenever the possibility of abolishing marriage is mentioned, people immediately cry, 'But what about the children?' The average person's first reaction is to assume that children would be worse off. Many couples who have been unhappily married for years claim that they stay together 'for the sake of the children'. Similarly, hundreds of thousands of women have got married when pregnant, so that they can give their child 'a proper home' and a traditional two-parent upbringing.

It is also often assumed that, but for marriage, a huge proportion of men would try to evade their responsibilities and not look after their wives or children. The holy estate of matrimony was ordained, according to the marriage service, primarily for the procreation of children, and, by implication, to ensure that any children will be brought up in a secure, loving (Christian) home with two caring parents. Marriage and children have always been upheld as the Christian ideal, as they are in many other religions. But there is a huge discrepancy between the ideal and the reality. Not everyone can make the falling-in-love/ marriage/home/children concept work, which explains why there are very many more unhappy than happy families. And not all couples who marry and set up home make good parents. Inside many traditional homes may be found parents who are cruel, uncaring, vicious, bad-tempered, violent, unloving and irresponsible. Any child who has loving, responsible, mature, intelligent parents, who are good providers and take the task of bringing up a family seriously, may count himself, or herself, lucky, for such parents are in the minority.

Unholy Matrimony

Moreover, the evidence all around us does little to suggest that today's typical family unit is producing happy, healthy, well-adjusted children. It is my belief that the 'happy family' of today is largely a myth, and that far more people are clustered together in misery than in happiness.

The overriding problem, surely, is that marriage and children *are* perceived as an ideal, as something to which everybody should aspire. Most people imagine they have a God-given right to find a life-long partner, get married and procreate. Children are seen as the natural outcome of marriage, the inevitable result of a man and woman's love for each other. Where and how this idea arose is unclear.

Children, unfortunately, are seen as universally desirable. Whenever a member of the royal family, a pop star or other celebrity has a baby, every newspaper carries pictures, often describing the baby in such terms as 'a bundle of joy'. We are encouraged to regard children as enhancers of our own happiness, as something which, after we have found a life-long partner, will complete us as human beings and bring us lasting bliss. It seems likely that one of the main reasons for the prevalence of post-natal depression is the great discrepancy between the fantasy and the reality. New mothers are expected – and themselves expect – to become suffused with love for their new offspring, but very many women do *not* feel unbounded love sweeping over them at this time. Nor, it must be said, do many new fathers. Some parents never experience the love they are supposed to, and feel constantly guilty as a result.

Linda in Nancy Mitford's *The Pursuit of Love* is a mother who does not love her newborn child. When Fanny, the narrator of the story, goes to see Linda in hospital, she is told: 'It's really kinder not to look.' Linda herself never looks at the baby if she can help it, and her feelings remain unchanged as the child grows up. Such unmaternal feelings are in fact quite common, but few women are as honest as the fictional Linda. Unfortunately we have all been so brainwashed into believing that marriage and children are a universal ideal for everybody, the one inevitably leading to the other, that few of us can make objectives decisions about them.

So what about the children?

I am convinced that if we did not see marriage and children as universally desirable we would be more inclined to stop and ask ourselves why we were begetting children and how we were going to look after these extra people in our lives. Most of us have children because we believe that they are somehow going to 'crown' our love for each other, to make it deeper and more significant, and, above all, because everybody else does.

Increasing numbers of people claim that they 'desperately' want children: they feel they have a right to them, as they imagine they have a right to any consumer item – refrigerator, car, fitted carpets or the latest hi-fi. And yet, as people more and more tend to assume they have a God-given right to have children, child abuse of various kinds appears to be greatly on the upturn. Even if, as some people claim, it is not so much on the increase as being reported more frequently, the numbers of abused children are still disturbingly large. Considerable numbers of them are taken into care every year, and most of these have been abused or ill-treated by their own parents – the very people who, from a biological standpoint, are supposed to be best qualified to bring them up. The problem is particularly common in Western society, where the 'love, marriage and children' pattern is promulgated as an ideal.

A great many young people now turn to drugs, many of them because they are seriously unhappy. It has been suggested, without any proper evidence to support the argument, that one of the main reasons why so many young people are on drugs, or are falling foul of the law, is because they come from 'broken homes'. Yet this accounts for only a minority. Most young drug-takers come from what we would consider traditional homes, where mother, father and children live together.

More children than ever before suffer from problems as diverse as dyslexia, hyperactivity, anorexia, eczema and asthma – all conditions which, if not caused by, are certainly exacerbated by unhappiness. Yet most of these children come from conventional two-parent families, in which the mother and father are married to each other and by whom the children were very much 'wanted'. Although the blame for young people's problems is often laid at the door of those who eschew traditional marriage and try to bring children up in other types of families, statistics (for example, those from the survey carried out by the National Children's Bureau in the late 1970s) show that almost all cases of behavioural problems occur in the kind of home that is blessed and endorsed by modern society.

The fantasy scenario for this ideal family unit is that a year or two after meeting, falling in love, marrying and setting up home together, the couple starts a family and has two children, probably in rapid succession. As parents, they jointly decide that two children are enough, and henceforth devote their time and energies to bringing up their offspring as best they can. The wife gives up her job and devotes herself to bringing up the children, at least while they are small, keeping at the back of her mind the possibility of a part-time job later which she can fit in with the children's routine. Meanwhile the husband prospers in his job, the couple begins to be able to afford foreign holidays, they move to a bigger house, get a second car and a few pets and live happily ever after.

Thus runs the pattern of the 'traditional', 'ideal' family. Almost every survey ever carried out suggests that this is the kind of family most people would like, or would like to have come from, with a dependable, hard-working father and a mother who is always on hand, always smiling, baking apple pies, smoothing down sheets and kissing grazed knees better; the children are well-scrubbed, well-fed, well-disciplined, do their homework and get good marks at school. In this fantasy home, there is always plenty of food in the house, everything is always clean, Mum and Dad are never in bad moods and the whole family has lots of fun together.

The trouble is that when people try to bring this fantasy to life, they often find things go badly wrong. For one thing, the parents may not be as blissfully content with each other as the TV ads and upholders of 'traditional' values would have us believe. Mum may resent being the household drudge, incarcerated at home, and Dad may resent the fact that every penny of his income is accounted for long before he earns it; he may not like his job, and

So what about the children?

he may have long since fallen out of love with his wife. For a time, the couple may try to maintain the pretence that everything is wonderful – after all, both have what they always wanted, don't they?

But it cannot be done. Frictions and resentments will start to become apparent in this dream house, notwithstanding all its material comforts. Added to which, the children may not turn out to be quite the paragons that were expected. Instead of being bright, affectionate, happy and healthy, they may be a disappointment: not very pretty, not all that clever, not in the least loving and liable to answer back and disobey. There is no guarantee that even the most wanted child of the most perfect couple will turn out a credit to the parents.

Parents easily feel let down by their children and can find it hard to love them. Moreover, many parents simply do not know what love means, because they equate loving with ownership; as the children grow up, their parents start to feel that they are owed something for all the hard work they have put in and the sacrifices they have made – sacrifices which the children never asked for, and which may serve only to put an additional burden on them. The problem stems from the fact that, for all too many people nowadays, children are seen as just another acquisition, something to show off and boast about.

Marriage and children are seen as so integral, so necessary to people's lives that few can ever imagine going through life without either. As both are seen, quite erroneously, to be providers of happiness and fulfilment, we feel thwarted and disappointed when neither marriage nor children fulfil us. But how can they? How can yoking yourself to another person for life possibly be personally 'fulfilling'? And even if it is, is such fulfilment a worthy goal? Surely the greatest fulfilment possible is that which comes from *self*-growth and *self*-development. Other people serve to hinder rather than encourage this.

If marriage arrests personal growth and stops people fully realizing their individual potential, consider how much greater this danger must be with children. All too many people take responsibility for instigating new human lives before they have learned how to handle their own. We foolishly imagine that marriage and children are going to make better people of us, extend and enrich our personalities and enable us to achieve maturity. Unfortunately, this cannot happen. We can only become mature if we spend time working out who we are, what we want to do and how we are going to achieve our objectives.

By far the great majority of people fall into marriage and family life in a kind of miasma, a cloud of romance and unreality, having very little idea of what they are doing. Formerly, few people had much choice in the matter. You grew up, you got married and, as a direct consequence, you had children – usually uninvited, but by no means always unwanted, for all that. In fact there is some evidence to suggest that in the days when children were not planned they were actually more welcome than they are today. Nowadays an increasing number of people want to have children, but do not want their lives to be disrupted as a result. They particularly do not want their children to cramp their social life or mess up their homes, their pale beige carpets or their upholstered furniture.

Children, it must be admitted, can be a nuisance. In many traditional homes, one in which the father goes out to work to earn the money and the mother stays at home, children are a constant source of irritation to the parents – they who have, after all, done what society told them they ought to do, and yet find they are not happy. Their marriage has not brought them happiness and neither have their children. As the years go by horizons become narrowed; for women, life may easily be reduced to a dreary domestic round and they can find their whole day taken up with tasks for which they have neither heart nor aptitude – ferrying children, cooking, cleaning, having their offspring's little friends to tea. Freedom has gone and what has replaced it seems very irksome. In addition, children are very expensive. If the woman has given up her job, the couple's income will have fallen dramatically, yet, at the same time, the demands of the children will be growing, and probably stretching financial resources to the limit.

This, it seems to me, is the reality of the 'happy family' of today. I have watched many of my friends, people who were dashing, adventurous, interesting, zany, become boring and dull after children entered their lives. This is not always the case, of course, but there is an inherent danger that it will happen once family life overtakes people.

David Pithers of the National Children's Home is certain that Britain, America and Canada are nations of child-haters. He sees the results of the fantasy that children are going to enhance adult lives in the Home, to which thousands of unwanted and neglected children find their way each year. A psychologist who has decided not to have children of his own, he feels that people today have children for completely the wrong reasons. Whereas in the past couples had children for dynastic purposes, or to help on the land, now the main reason is that they think their children will love them. We are all so hungry for love that we expect the baby to which we have just given birth to love us, instantly.

Of course, the baby does not give love, but only wants to receive it. According to David Pithers, it is when the parents perceive this that the trouble starts. They may then begin to reject the child, who cries, makes demands and is simultaneously curtailing both the freedom and the income of the parents. It seems that children give very little in return for so large a sacrifice by the parents. In extreme cases, this may lead to their abusing the child, so great is their disappointment.

It is commonly believed that, in order to grow up properly, a child must always have both parents around. One-parent families are seen, even nowadays, as something to be avoided if at all possible. They are generally poorer than two-parent ones, after all, and the single parent may be under extra strain, having to do the job of both parents. But is one parent really obliged to try to do the job of two? In large numbers of traditional homes with two parents the father does precious little parenting. Many high-achieving fathers see hardly anything of their children. Yet nobody would say that such children come from 'broken homes'. By far the great majority of children who grow up in homes where there are two parents are virtually from one-parent families, because the father takes no part at all in their upbringing. Many men imagine that if they earn enough money and provide a big house replete with consumer luxuries, they are doing their job as parents. Can the ever-absent father, in such cases, be said to be providing a good role model for his children? The most that can be said is that such parents keep the patriarchal nature of today's family intact.

Some men have an extremely perverted idea of what love is and how it should be displayed between parents and children. In the numerous child abuse cases which have come to light over the past few years it has been, almost without exception, the father abusing the child. Often, but by no means always, it is the girls who are abused. The father tries to persuade the child to show her 'love' by taking part in sexual or semi-sexual activities. When the child refuses, or is frightened, the father may force the issue.

Sometimes the mother truly does not know what is going on, but this seems unlikely in the majority of cases. Commonly she knows about the situation but says nothing and does nothing. There are several reasons why. One is that, even today, many women are very frightened of the men with whom they live. They dare not do anything that could cause trouble, largely because they have no independent income and nowhere to go if a major row should ensue. The mother may also be relieved that while the father is bothering the child sexually he is not bothering her. At least *she* has escaped. Apart from this, many women know that if the case were to come to court the father would very probably be sent to prison, and then the whole family would suffer even more.

It is often imagined that abuse takes place only in chaotic homes, where the woman has several children by different men, and the abuser is just her latest boyfriend. This happens, of course, but in common with other family problems the majority of abuse takes place in 'respectable' two-parent homes, where the adults are married to each other.

Over the past few years evidence has accumulated to indicate that matrimonial homes, far from being havens of peace and love, are often hotbeds of resentment, rage and cruelty in which the individuals are unhappy with each other and do not like each other very much. Homes in which teenagers do not speak to their parents, or are rude and thoughtless, are so common that we have come to see uncouth behaviour by young people as the norm, as a 'stage they are going through'. Homes in which the mother and father constantly complain about each other to the children are also extremely common.

It seems that we are paying a very high price for buying a fantasy.

So how would abolition of state marriage give children a vastly better deal? In the first place, the idea that women should be economically dependent on men would end. Children would no longer grow up, as they still do today, with the understanding that males are superior to females. Conventional homes – the ones to which society thinks everyone should aspire – undeniably perpetuate the patriarchal notion that the man is more important, that it is his line, his name, which must be continued, and that it is directly due to his efforts that the whole family is kept together, housed, fed, clothed and shod.

Marriage, as currently constituted, has at its very heart the concept of male superiority. As long as we retain a sentimental picture of marriage, we are preserving the idea that men are superior. Indeed, we cannot ensure the sexes are treated equally while we continue to 'honour' marriage. Only by abolishing marriage could we achieve that. This would put paid to the fallacy, of both fantasy and fact, that a home is not a real home without a male breadwinner. If all women and all men were eternally single in law, then the patriarchy, which oppresses and diminishes women by its very nature, would vanish. Women's dependency upon men would disappear, and thereafter, forever, there would be fewer cases of child abuse, fewer couples staying together 'for the sake of the children' and fewer women frightened to stand up to men. Economic independence could achieve all this for women and for the children of the future.

If women remain single in law, they will automatically become eligible for all the state benefits which at the moment are denied to them as married women. Abolition of the married couple's allowance would release large sums of money which could be diverted to women who are forgoing the chance of an independent income to bring up their children. The £7.25 per child weekly benefit would no longer be their only 'independent' income, because they would be eligible for *all* state benefits, whether or not they are cohabiting.

This idea in fact amounts to paying women who stay at home to look after children a proper wage. In practical terms nothing would alter except that such women would no longer be dependent on a man. It would not mean that no families would include an adult male. All the studies which have been carried out on cohabiting, as opposed to formally married, couples suggest that these unions are as solid and long-lasting as their married equivalents. They may even last longer: because the union is, in Shelley's words, more free and equal, couples stay together out of mutual regard, not because they have no alternative.

If women know that they can, indeed must, be economically independent forever, girls will be able to grow up with a far greater sense of self-worth than they have at present. Boys, too, will grow up learning that if they want respect, and to be superior, they will have to earn such status, and that it is not theirs by right of gender.

The abolition of marriage will also have the happy result that children will not see their father as the more important parent. Obituaries in the press often mention the male antecedents of the recently deceased, but hardly ever is there any reference to the mother – the person who gave birth to this latterly illustrious figure and, most probably, brought him or her up. Because female lines are automatically lost on marriage, women are perpetually being wiped out. Women have been largely deleted from history thanks to marriage, because on marriage their names disappear.

When couples cohabit, rather than marry, it is common for the children to take the name of the father even though they are illegitimate. Even here patriarchy rules. If marriage did not exist, the idea that only male lines were worth preserving would also vanish. Children would be able to take either the mother's or the father's name. Some avant-garde families give boys the father's surname, girls the mother's. It has been argued, in favour of

So what about the children?

continuing patriarchal names, that even women's names are men's, in that they are the father's rather than the mother's. Abolition of marriage would bring an immediate end to this.

It is still an almost universal practice for children to take the name of the father rather than the mother. In some countries, such as Iceland, Poland and the USSR, surnames are feminized, but they are still basically the man's name. Most wives automatically take their husbands' surnames on marriage, never even considering the option of not doing so. This paves the way for the children 'naturally' to take the father's name.

All this reinforces the idea that women are not as important as men, that they are the dependent, passive sex.

If marriage were abolished, there would be no differences whatever between illegitimate and legitimate children. Throughout the ages, especially in royal and aristocratic circles, it has been considered extremely important for all heirs to be legitimate – born within wedlock. But of course there is nothing 'natural' in all this – legitimacy and illegitimacy laws have been formulated by men, just as marriage laws have. People have suffered greatly in the past from the stigma of being labelled a bastard, and the mother is commonly held to be responsible.

In *One-Parent Families*, a book written to raise funds for the excellent National Council for One-Parent Families, a variety of writers and thinkers give their views on what it means to be a bastard, and what the legitimacy laws have meant to women and children. Eva Figes, thinking of the sad plight of Thomas Hardy's Tess of the d'Urbervilles, writes: 'The spectre of becoming an unmarried mother became [for women of that era] an invisible chastity belt.'

She goes on:

> I came to realize [after her own marriage had ended] that society not only stunted and frustrated the would-be 'career girl' but exploited all women in the most fundamental way, and that the lip service which this society paid to the high ideals of marriage, family life and parenthood, particularly responsible parenthood, was a total hypocrisy. The married woman has no rights and no dignity except those which her husband is pleased to confer on her. If she is rejected, through no fault of her own,

Unholy Matrimony

she and her children go right to the bottom of the social heap. . . . Nothing will really change until the economic bond of marriage is broken.

These words were written in 1973, and nothing has changed, except that unmarried mothers are no longer as stigmatized as they were, largely thanks to the campaigning work of One-Parent Families, the charity formed in 1918 as The National Council for the Unmarried Mother and Her Child.

In this same book, other writers say that single mothers have felt themselves becoming more aggressive and 'masculine' once their economic bondage to a man ceased. The book also maintains that, contrary to dire predictions from traditionalists, the family unit is not on its way out, but is encouraged at every turn by society, the law and so-called upholders of tradition.

Sheila Hancock, the actress, writes:

I rather question the overriding importance of a mother's and a father's influence on a child. I have seen so many examples of awful parents that children would be better off without. I mourn the passing of those huge family set-ups where you spent as much time with Gran and Uncle and neighbours as with Mum.

The novelist Brigid Brophy makes the point that Christianity, which is largely responsible for the marriage service, and the wording of the marriage laws, has at its head a bastard. Jesus was, strictly speaking, born out of wedlock: he was not the son of his mother's husband. Brophy goes on to say that marriage is in any case a purely human invention: animals have no marriage laws, therefore, logically, all animals are 'bastards'.

The reason why bastardy matters, Brigid Brophy writes, is money. In the past, if a child was illegitimate, he or she could not inherit the father's title, property or wealth. The mother's title, property and wealth were hardly worth inheriting. It was the father's name and lineage which were important.

The standard parental unit of one-plus-one, rigidly divided into seller-of-sexual-favours and earner-of-bread-to-pay-for-them, has not been, declares Brophy, such a runaway success that we should suppress individual departures from it. The existence of a matrimonial home does not necessarily safeguard a child's bodily well-being. It may be even less reliable as a safeguard of society's and our species' future.

'It may well be,' writes Brophy, 'that the tensions, frustrations and irrational loyalty of the two-parent unit have been translated into the nationalisms and belligerence of our world society.'

Indeed, to impose a single pattern is not only to defy the individuality of parents but to defy, in advance of their birth, the individuality of children. The argument that 'nature' intends a child to have two parents is, like all arguments from biological fact to normative judgement, nonsense where humans are concerned. . . . Some babies can be excellently cared for by one parent with only half a mind on the job, whereas others, had nature indeed been wise and providential, would have been begotten by four fathers and conceived by four mothers.

If there were no state form of marriage, the way would be opened for many more different types of union to come into being, and this could only be to the advantage of children. At the moment, although increasing numbers of people are deciding to deviate from the two-parent family unit, other types of family are considered wrong. For instance, it is considered wrong for two people acting as parents to be of the same sex, yet certain lesbian women are deciding to have babies by artificial insemination and then to bring them up with two mothers rather than a mother and a father.

Lesbian parents I have spoken to say that it is very easy to become pregnant by means of do-it-yourself AID (artificial insemination by donor): self-insemination is often successful after only one or two sessions. The biological father may never know that his sperm has fathered a child, and will have no involvement with the child apart from being the provider of the sperm. Some of these AID children are now seven and eight years old and are certainly just as much loved and cared for as any child from a heterosexual unit. The advantage with lesbian couples is that the rigid sexual division into carer and breadwinner does not exist. The tasks are shared and, of course, the parents can take turns at looking after the child and earning money.

Unholy Matrimony

There was a huge outcry when the book *Jenny Lives with Eric and Martin* was published, because it depicted a small girl growing up in a homosexual home. Yet it implied that the home was loving and caring, and that the two gay men put a lot of thought into how to bring up a child. Traditionalists said that this was wrong, that it was going against nature and should not be encouraged. But, as Brigid Brophy has observed, the two-parent family unit of biological mother and father has not been such a runaway success that we should automatically rule out alternatives.

Single women are increasingly deciding to have children by an anonymous donor rather than a sexual partner. A donor, who simply provides sperm, has no rights whatever to the child, and cannot claim custody or have any say in his or her upbringing. All the evidence available so far suggests that these children, who are supremely wanted, and who are conceived without any sexual act having taken place or any intimate relationship having existed between the couple, do not suffer in any way at all.

Linda Edwards, a university lecturer who decided to have a baby by artificial, or 'alternative', insemination (practitioners point out that this form of insemination is not 'artificial' and should no longer be called such), outlined the reasons for her decision in an interview in *The Independent* in December 1987. When she first decided she wanted a child, she advertised in the magazine *City Limits*, saying that she was one of a group of women who had chosen to live independently of men but wanted to have children. She added that she intended to do this by self-insemination, to ensure that she had 'complete control over [her] fertility'. The advertisement, calling for a suitable donor, stated that the man would have to ejaculate into a clean receptacle – and that would be all that was required of him.

Having found a suitable donor, Linda worked out when she was due to ovulate so that the donor would be ready to ejaculate in the next room when the time was right. As the sperm lives only for about three hours, and has to be kept at a certain temperature, timing is crucial. She became pregnant in the fourth month of trying, and her son Jay was two years old at the time she gave the interview.

So what about the children?

She said:

Although I can see disadvantages for Jay in terms of [my] not being a father, I think that I'm bringing him up well and he's getting lots of other things . . . I think he's probably had more men around than most kids because his childminder for nearly a year was a man. And Barry, my ex-husband, is involved with him as well . . .

I think what is important is how good a parent you are . . . If the relationship between parents and child is tension-free, I don't think it matters whether it's the mother on her own or the father on his own.

Linda Edwards added that she was not exactly bringing the child up on her own, as are many unmarried mothers, because plenty of other people were always at hand. This was a deliberate policy, and neither was lonely or isolated.

The law at present states that children of parents who are not married, who are born of surrogate mothers or by artificial insemination, are illegitimate. For some reason, illegitimacy does not apply to adopted children. And children can only be formally adopted where there are two parents of different sexes who are married to each other.

The so-called stigma of illegitimacy has been cited as a potent reason for all parents to marry. But before very long all the differences between legitimate and non-legitimate children will be swept away by law. The only reason that illegitimacy laws have lasted so long is that society has continued to uphold the married, two-parent family as the only responsible way to bring up children.

Now that illegitimacy laws are fast disappearing, there is even less reason to preserve the concept of marriage. In the past, undoubtedly, many couples married simply because the woman was pregnant. This was certainly happening as recently as the 'sixties and 'seventies and is probably still happening. Sometimes women would deliberately get themselves pregnant just so their men would marry them, in the days when a woman's status was thought to be enhanced by marriage. It was a dangerous thing to do, of course, because very often the man took fright and refused to marry the girlfriend – and then she would be left high and dry with a baby she did not really want.

Unholy Matrimony

In Britain illegitimacy is vastly on the increase. A report in the *Journal of the Royal College of General Practitioners* (November 1987) stated that 36 per cent of conceptions in England and Wales now occur outside marriage, as compared with 23 per cent in 1975; the report described these as 'startling' figures. However, far from suggesting a rising tide of immorality, the figures provide an insight into changing attitudes towards marriage and the stigma of illegitimacy. From 1975 to 1985, the report states, the proportion of illegitimate conceptions that were followed by marriage and legitimate maternity fell from 26 to 15 per cent. At the same time the proportion of children registered in joint names (indicating a stable relationship) rose from 17 to 32 per cent. About three-quarters of the parents registering births gave a single address for registration.

These statistics indicate that people are deciding for themselves, in even greater numbers, that they do not want to get married, even when they have children. 'Living together' now has no stigma at all and 'illegitimacy' has lost virtually all of its previous bad associations. It is often hard to realize just how quickly these changes have taken place. When I was a student in the 1960s, considerable numbers of my female friends became pregnant and got married ('had to get married', in the phrase of the time) at the age of nineteen or twenty. The pregnancies were not intended, and simply served to damage their academic careers, as well as their future professional careers. Some won through in the end, others just wilted under the unfairness of it all. The young men concerned did not seem to suffer greatly – except that they were to a certain extent 'tied down' by marriage. Now those unplanned babies have become adults themselves, and it seems that in the vast number of cases their parents divorced years ago.

It is unlikely that this new generation would get married simply because of pregnancy. They would not see the point. But as the report in the GPs' *Journal* shows, illegitimacy no longer means lone parenthood, poverty or being cast out of the family home. By far the great majority of illegitimate children nowadays have two parents who live together, are equally devoted to the child's welfare, and are to all intents and purposes as much a couple as if they had got married.

The National Council for One-Parent families has played a major part in getting illegitimacy laws changed. The Family Law Reform Act will remove most of the existing legal discrimination against children born outside marriage. (The Council rejects the word 'illegitimate' owing to its pejorative associations.) The informing principle of these legal reforms is that the marital status of their parents is irrelevant to children. The question of inheritance will no longer pose problems for the child of unmarried parents: he or she will be able to inherit in just the same way as children of married parents. Unmarried fathers may apply to share parental rights and apply for guardianship, if necessary.

In the past an illegitimate child was considered in law to belong to the mother only, and the father had no rights. This law was probably passed to allow men to evade their responsibilities towards children born to them out of wedlock, but as attitudes became more liberal, fathers increasingly felt they did not want to be left out – and that they actually wanted to play a proper part in the upbringing of their children.

Angela Hadjipateras of One-Parent Families says: 'This new Act will remove practically every single form of discrimination now operating against illegitimate children. The only thing that so far has not changed is the question of nationality. Illegitimacy laws still apply to children whose parents are not British.'

Other countries, similarly, have mitigated the differences between legitimate and illegitimate children. The unattractiveness of single parenthood – rendered thus largely by harsh laws – is now fading all across Europe and America. In many Latin American and African countries illegitimacy has in any case always been extremely common, and many relationships are of a highly casual nature.

As the law now stands in several countries, children of cohabiting couples enjoy many of the rights formerly enjoyed only by the offspring of the legally married. The father is seen as having a duty to provide for his children, and if a woman has sacrificed her career for motherhood she is entitled to maintenance. In theory, the opposite also applies; if a man decides to give up his job to bring up the children of a former relationship, his ex-cohabitee may be ordered to pay maintenance. In Sweden, the Parents' and Children's Code of 1978 recognizes that there are mutual financial obligations in non-marital relationships. Also, if one cohabitant is not economically active, Swedish pension law makes appropriate allowance for this. In most countries it is still the case that the mother has slightly more rights than the father over a child born out of wedlock, and is likely to be granted legal custody.

The high incidence of children born to cohabiting couples has meant that in many countries the law has tended to approximate more and more to that of marriage, and in some cases is almost indistinguishable. It aims, laudably, to protect the children, but, notwithstanding, cohabitation laws are following those for marriage in that, where children exist, women's economic dependency upon men is assumed, and even encouraged. Yet again, it is taken for granted that the presence of children means that somebody has to become non-earning. The concept is so deeply embedded in our consciousness that it has survived other dramatic changes in social attitudes. Although I am in favour of either a state wage, or state benefits of a high enough level to live on, for people who are bringing up children and not working, I do not think people should be economically inactive just because there are children around.

It should be possible to devise a system which allows people to carry on their careers if they want to, while knowing that their children are well cared for. This happens, after all, in the kibbutz system in Israel, where both parents carry on working after their children are born. The children are looked after by trained nurses and staff in baby houses and kindergartens. It used to be the case that babies were separated from their parents, even sleeping in the baby houses. Now, in many kibbutzim, they are allowed home at night. But in all of them both parents know that their children are being well cared for by qualified nurses and teachers and can rest assured that they will come to no harm. The children probably

So what about the children?

benefit enormously by not coming from a too-close, too-intimate and exclusive family unit.

It should be perfectly possible to set up good day nurseries, staffed by properly qualified people, where children can be left and be well looked after. For many, many years, people in Britain have bemoaned the lack of nurseries – which, after all, *did* exist during the Second World War, when women were needed to work. One of the reasons why they no longer exist is because women are not sure they are doing the right thing by leaving their children. To have children *and* do an interesting job would be like having too much: independence at too low a price; too much heady freedom. Children nowadays act as jailers and we are not making much effort to change the situation. There is no good reason why proper nurseries should not be set up everywhere, and no good reason why school-age children should not have somewhere to go until their parents come home from work. Only an outdated ideology stops these places being set up on a proper basis. Society still has lingering doubts about those mothers who employ nannies and go out to work in proper, well paid jobs. There is even more unease when people realize that the offspring of such mothers do not suffer at all, but are often brighter, happier and better behaved than those of 'professional', full-time mothers.

The question of what would happen to the children if both parents went out to work has been much discussed, as if it were an insuperable problem. The guilt of working mothers is also encouraged. The guilt-inducing philosophy is intended to make women worried and nervous about what they are doing. We do not encourage female independence. Our own mothers discourage it, because few of them ever had such freedom and they do not want their daughters to have it either. The attitude of 'I went through it – so should you' dies hard.

But if the whole concept of marriage and economic dependency were to disappear, women would have a very different attitude towards childbirth, paid employment, and themselves. Instead of fitting jobs round the baby, they would fit the baby round the job. This would enable everybody to become more productive and self-sufficient. Women would also stop looking towards children for their fulfilment, and would start to depend upon themselves. This might mean fewer children being born, but it would also mean that parents would not have unrealistic expectations of their children. If people had children only when they really cherished the responsibility of looking after them into adulthood, and not to revivify dying relationships, to escape a bad home or a boring job, or because they felt unloved and unwanted, then there would be far fewer problem children and problem families.

At the moment most people believe they have a perfect right to have children, in much the same way that they believe they have a right to a home and an income. But who gives us that right? Nobody ever checks to see whether we are fit to be parents and no government would ever dare to legislate for such a system of qualification. When Hitler tried to ensure, in Germany, that only perfect, non-handicapped children should be born, the rest of the world reacted in horror to this fascist idea.

Parental selection cannot be imposed from above outside a dictatorial, totalitarian regime, but if we were all brought up to recognize that children are a huge responsibility, not an automatic right and never to be undertaken lightly, better parents would result.

I'm afraid I have little sympathy for those infertile couples who 'desperately' want children. They should be putting the question the other way round and asking whether the children desperately want *them*. Instead of mindlessly longing for a child, people should ask themselves what they could offer a child, and whether this is enough to justify bringing another human being into the world. Some people, of course, make ideal parents – but the biological capability of producing a baby does not automatically confer this talent. Nor do people become mature, or better, more responsible human beings, just because they have a child to look after. In some cases people are made better by having children, but by no means always. The biggest danger is that, having had them, the parents will try to treat their children as possessions.

It used to be said that people who do not want children are selfish. In fact, it is those who *do* want them who are selfish,

So what about the children?

because they rarely want them for good reasons. By bringing children into the world they are adding to its problems, not reducing them.

One mother I spoke to told me that her children had enhanced her life. But does that justify her having had them? Having children has to be seen as one-way traffic. You may love them, but you cannot expect them to love you. You may do everything possible for them, but you can never expect them to be grateful, or to feel they owe you anything. Parents should also be ready to let their children fly the nest when they have grown up, and never to put emotional burdens or obligations on them.

Relationships between parents and children are often very bad nowadays, mainly because people have children for the wrong reasons. That doesn't mean, of course, that children are never loved. Several writers, Germaine Greer and Marilyn French among them, have drawn attention to the fact that many mothers are prepared to do anything for their children. In many cases, the only real love in an individual's life is that for his or her children, for this is unstinting and does not seek reward. Many people who have had children feel intense love for the first time in their lives, regardless of whether that love is returned. In such a way children can bring out some of the very finest human instincts (but they can also bring out the worst).

Before having children, people of either sex should ask themselves, 'Is there any way I can look after this child without becoming dependent on somebody else? If the answer is no, then they should seriously consider whether they are doing the right thing. In the past, when contraception was either unreliable or non-existent, this question could not have been asked. Now it can. And now, moreover, there can be no real justification for anybody to be economically dependent. It is wrong, and should be seen as such.

Of course, if there were no marriage, there would be no divorce, and this would be an unequivocally good thing. Divorce is still seen as adversarial, the result of the 'irretrievable breakdown' of marriage, and the legal profession tends to assume that the once-married couple now hate each other. In many cases they do not hate each other at all but merely want to lead separate lives. Yet if they try to arrange a divorce, they will find that one has to be a petitioner and the other a respondent. Divorce in its present form is undignified and, like marriage, is based on the premise that women must be economically dependent upon men. Women are still entitled, under the law, to claim maintenance after a divorce, even if there is no reason for them to expect an income. Nowadays, men can also do this.

In most divorces which involve children, the children always suffer the most. Marriage nowadays patently does not guarantee a safe and stable home or that any children will be brought up by two parents. Many one-parent homes today are establishments in which there has been a formal marriage but the marriage has come apart, rather than those consisting of a mother plus 'illegitimate' children.

If marriage did not exist there would be no reason why people who wish to cohabit and have children should not be lesbian or gay, or even threesomes and foursomes rather than couples. But before bringing another human being into the world, would-be parents should seriously consider their financial, legal and moral responsibilities and then draw up a legally binding agreement, subject to regular reviews as circumstances changed, thus cutting down the adversarial aspect of maintenance and access if the relationship should break up. Nobody can ever guarantee that a relationship will last. The more restrictive the laws, the more unhappiness will be created.

Partnerships in which children exist, or may exist in the future, would greatly benefit from being regarded as a business contract. There is, however, no one form of contract which would suit everybody, and that is why they would have to be individual. The main problem with both marriage and cohabitation laws is that they try to impose one set of rules on everybody, regardless of individual differences. There will never be a single set of conditions which applies to every case.

The contract should, however, cover mutual duties, obligations and responsibilities, and its guiding principle should be that the welfare of any child born to the couple is paramount. This is in fact what courts try to do today, but they fail miserably owing to the legal straitjacket that currently obtains.

As for *any* contract, mutually agreed terms should be the watchword. These would have to make provision for the children in the event of the relationship breaking up: who would take responsibility for them, financial arrangements, and so on. If the terms are acceptable to both parties and do not contravene the law, the contract should be considered binding until such time as it is mutually agreed that changes are necessary.

Critics of such a plan might feel that the binding contact essentially removes the concepts of love and freedom from any relationship involving children. However, there is little freedom in the present system of marriage and divorce, which is beset by outdated laws and customs that are often not in the best interests of the people concerned.

If, additionally, couples wish to make vows of commitment in church, or in some other sacred place, that would be their right.

The system I am proposing would make it essential for those concerned to think, deeply, about the nature of their commitment to another person, and to consider fully the implications of bringing children into the world. The individually tailored contract would force people to examine their relationship and their desire for a family more fully than is necessary at present and could therefore go some way to preventing the misery that currently tends to overtake both.

9

The ritualization of marriage

In virtually every country in the world weddings are an occasion for huge spending and huge celebration. At the time of writing, the average wedding in the UK costs about £4000. The idea of the 'white wedding' with its attendant fuss and bother is becoming standard even in countries where there is no Christian tradition.

According to a survey in the magazine *Wedding and Home*, in Britain getting married is the second biggest expense after buying a home. Average expenditure is as follows: £250 for an engagement ring; £76 for the wedding ring; £300 for the dress, veil and shoes; £180 for bridesmaids' dresses; £125 for the bridegroom's suit; £100 for flowers; over £100 for hire cars.

In addition, the photographer costs another £150, a video to mark the occasion about £130, and the reception at least £1000. The average number of guests is just over 100. The honeymoon is another major expense, costing an average of £820 for eleven days (flights and accommodation).

The sums mentioned in the survey were for an average wedding, not a particularly grand one. In *Brides* magazine wedding dresses are currently priced at £600 or more. The featured gowns are, without doubt, exquisitely made, very much one-offs, rather than mass-produced, so that the bride can feel really special on what is normally perceived as her big day. Also on display are suitable outfits for the mother of the bride, which frequently cost several hundred pounds each.

Weddings are a major industry nowadays. Considerable numbers of people make very good livings out of weddings, and the range of goods and services on offer multiplies all the time.

Unholy Matrimony

Make-up experts and hairdressers who come to the bride's home can be hired, and there is a growing number of companies which exist to arrange video-taping of the whole proceedings – a procedure that is now becoming *de rigueur*. There are also firms who will undertake to arrange the whole wedding, from start to finish, including dresses, flowers, cars, reception and so on.

Even though this is all so much money down the drain, nobody seems to think of it like that. Few people ever seem to ask themselves whether spending thousands of pounds on a lavish wedding is a good use of financial resources. However much weddings cost, and however much anxiety their planning causes, nobody ever seems to grudge the time or money spent.

In *Brides* magazine, the Bride's Wedding Guide (in each issue) advises beginning preparations at least three months in advance of the event, and then lists what everybody concerned must do, beginning with the announcement of the engagement in the local newspaper. As one might expect, this announcement is worded in patriarchal terms, with the man's name first and the female parent obliterated in both cases by being styled 'Mrs John Smith'. The same practice is followed on the invitations themselves. The *Brides* guide advises on the 'correct' form for invitations: if the parents are still married, 'Mr and Mrs Tom Baker' invite the guest to their daughter's wedding; if they are divorced it is 'Mr Tom Baker' and 'Mrs Eileen Baker'; and if the bride's mother has remarried, invitations are sent out by 'Mr and Mrs Harry Sinclair', if the stepfather is hosting the function. Etiquette demands that the man comes first wherever possible and that the woman is obliterated. Most people who send out wedding invitations are women; most people who arrange weddings are women; and the journalists on bridal magazines are mainly women: why do they allow this male dominance to continue – and then call it 'correct'? It is hard to see how a wedding can be a girl's 'big day' when she is doing her utmost to conform to a patriarchal tradition.

However, although women might arrange weddings, make the dresses and even do the catering, it is usually the man who pays, the grey man in the background without whom none of this would be possible. *Brides* magazine recently (December 1987) carried an article by a 'mother of the bride' who describes how she almost fainted in a dress shop at the price of a dress she liked, at which the assistant exclaimed: 'But it *is* for your daughter's wedding, is it not? What would a husband not pay for his wife to look wonderful on such a day?' The bride's mother acquiesced, seeming to regard it as perfectly all right for her husband to pay for the dress. Many brides' mothers would probably have felt the same.

Until women start to pay for weddings, out of their own earned income, nothing will change. Where weddings are concerned, women are truly back in the Dark Ages, acting as the 'token torturers' that Mary Daly talks about in *Gyn/Ecology*. While all the preparations for the maiden sacrifice are taking place, the men remain well out of it, coming to the fore only when there is a bill to be paid. The very dress of the men at a typical wedding – grey coat, top hat – makes them seem like accessories, bit players rather than the stars. The bride and her mother can come to the fore in pretty, expensive dresses on this one day because all know that for the rest of her life, the soon-to-be wife will be under the domination of a man.

There is hardly any more equality in marriage than ever there was, and the ceremony of the wedding makes this only too plain. Yet so many people are dazzled by the ceremonial aspect, the long white dress, the church, the solemn vows, the hymns and the no-expense-spared reception that they fail to see what is actually behind the ritual.

If weddings were, as they are supposed to be, merely an affirmation of two people's love and regard for each other, there would be no need to enshrine them in all this expensive and quite unnecessary ritual. You are no more married, in legal terms, if you have a huge ceremony than if you sneak off to a nearby registry office and grab a couple of witnesses off the street. It seems to me that any affirmation that henceforth two people are going to engage in compulsory sexual intercourse should be something very private. Moreover, one would think that the modern woman would want to hide the fact that she is 'giving' herself over to male ownership. But no, everybody seems to want to make the biggest, most public exhibition possible out of this decision. Perhaps they feel that the more ritual they engage in, the more this will hide what is really happening.

Most brides and grooms say afterwards that they can hardly remember a minute of their wedding – it all took place in a haze of unreality. Big weddings are often little better than an excuse for people to show off, to let others know how good they are at organizing, how rich they are, what an impressive do they can put on if necessary. Commonly, these are people who have never given themselves a chance to shine at anything else.

It does not take a brilliant brain to come to the conclusion that weddings are getting bigger, grander and more expensive in inverse proportion to the success of the actual marriage and relationship. The more lavish the wedding, the shorter and more acrimonious tends to be the marriage. By having a grand wedding, we are paying homage to the talismanic nature of ritual and ceremony. We put on peculiar clothes, such as are not normally worn, and go through procedures that are not part of everyday life, as if by doing so we can ward off the possibility that things will not work out later. The wedding service refers to divine love, togetherness, and asks the couple in front of the clergyman to make vows to each other which are virtually impossible to keep. Some brides and grooms never even consider sticking to the vows, yet a majority of people make them.

The service perpetuates the idea that the bride is passing from the ownership of the father to the ownership of the husband. Assets are being transferred, as in the days when marriage was basically a property transaction and the bride was considered an economic commodity just like land, a house or livestock.

The idea of giving the bride away is more than merely symbolic. Though only vestiges of the property transfer principle are retained in European marriages, the idea of ownership is quite literal in some countries. Sikh girls, for instance, are brought up from birth with the idea that they are owned for life, first by their fathers and then by their husbands, and they are schooled in obedience and passivity from their earliest years.

Everything else about weddings, even modern ones, strongly

echoes the ancient ritual of the virgin sacrifice. Though few brides are virgins nowadays, most still like to wear white dresses and a veil. They are being offered up to a man, as if the man were a god and worthy of a human sacrifice. This often happens even when the bride and groom may have been living together for some time before the ceremony. For the actual wedding, the bride becomes a virgin again, fresh, clean and new, offered up for her new husband to deflower and claim as his.

Weddings mask the reality of what is going to happen afterwards. In most wedding rituals throughout the world, it is the bride who takes centre stage, and it is she rather than the groom, who is groomed. In some countries the bride's 'superfluous' hair is shaved off; in others she is given massages for weeks beforehand; and in yet others she is given a specially exotic wedding make-up. It is unlikely that similar attention will be paid to the bridegroom's appearance. He is not obliged to prepare for his wedding by being bathed and perfumed in order to be worthy of his bride.

The belief that weddings are above all the bride's day, not the groom's, has probably arisen because we all know, though nobody ever says it, that for the rest of her life it will be he, her husband, who calls the tune. As soon as the ceremony is over, the radiant bride disappears into total anonymity, her individuality annihilated. It is common practice, when pieces of the wedding cake are sent out, for a little card to accompany the box saying, 'With the compliments of Mr and Mrs John Smith'. In the space of just a few weeks the radiant bride has become just another housewife, just another 'and Mrs', her 'special' day completely forgotten.

It is not really any sort of achievement to be marrying someone, yet we act as if it were. We like to plan ahead with military precision. Royal weddings are the ultimate occasions for ritual and ceremony, watched by millions and sometimes marked by a public holiday. We all love a wedding, especially a royal one. Weddings are, above all, supposed to celebrate the happiness of the couple being joined together. Yet when Edward VIII married Mrs Simpson, the world did not celebrate. We may like to mark

Unholy Matrimony

the happiness of the bridal pair, but only if they conform to preconceived ideas of what a couple should be – neither of them previously married and with no hint of a disreputable past. Yet in the UK there is a coming trend for second weddings to be almost as lavish and costly as the first, although the ceremony is different. It seems that the worse the chances of happiness in marriage, the more ostentatious the ceremonies we arrange.

Nowhere is this more noticeable than in the USA. When the Greek writer Arianna Stassinopoulos married Michael Huffington, a Texas oilman, she wore a £60,000 dress designed by Nancy Reagan's dressmaker and flashed a 60-carat engagement ring. At the age of 36 and with a somewhat eventful past, the bride still wore traditional white and carried a bouquet. Lavish weddings are not, however, the exclusive province of the rich and famous. In January 1986 an extremely expensive wedding took place in Washington DC to mark the joining together in matrimony of two people named Tami Hockestra and Juan Rocha. The bride's mother, who had decided that their wedding had to be the best ever, spent a total of £350,000 on the occasion. Afterwards, she walked into a bankruptcy court and announced that she could not possibly pay for the wedding, for which she had hired scores of violinists, 67 limousines, a yacht, and jets to transport the guests; she had also booked 110 rooms at the Sheraton Carlton for three days; £30,000 worth of flowers decorated the church, and the couple had a honeymoon booked at Disneyworld. Mrs Hockestra was not a rich woman: she ran a small cattle-feed business in Illinois and had apparently been in financial difficulties for some time. But she had wanted to give her daughter a wedding she would never forget. This she undoubtedly achieved – but at what true cost, and was it, in the end, a worthwhile financial investment?

In Japan nowadays wedding ceremonies are getting even more ridiculous: special effects that are becoming *de rigueur* include spotlights in seven colours and ethereal mists generated by dry ice; a master of ceremonies will ensure that all runs smoothly and the event will naturally be video-taped by professionals. The average bill for a Japanese wedding now stands at nearly £24,500

The ritualization of marriage

– more than 18 months' salary for a white-collar worker. This sum includes a certain amount of furniture and a particularly grand honeymoon (in Hawaii, for example, which would in itself cost over £3,000). A ceremony and reception costing almost £10,000 are now considered average (most receptions are for many more than 100 guests) and gifts are showered upon the couple at a cost of many thousands of pounds.

In India, too, wedding ceremonies are traditionally very lavish, and have become such a financial burden that parents now dread more than ever having girls, owing to the cost of their weddings and the dowries they must take to their husbands. Dowries are still common among Indian families. When the Maharajah of Gwalior's daughter married the son of the Maharajah of Kashmir in December 1987 a total of 50,000 people were invited to the wedding. Several hundred thousand pounds' worth of jewellery was exchanged and the townspeople of Gwalior were granted a public holiday. More than £250,000 was spent decorating the city. These maharajahs could no doubt afford such an outlay, but even rich families now hate having girls because they have to start saving up for their weddings from birth. Instead of giving girls a good education, which will enable them to earn their own living and not be dependent upon men, many parents keep all the money for their daughters' husbands' families, to be paid as a dowry. This does not happen in every family, however: and in some cases a girl's education is considered to add to her marriageability. Richer families often spend a lot of money nowadays on their daughters' education; some take degree after degree in order that they may attract a man who is both rich and educated. But however the money is spent, the object is to enhance the daughter's chances in the marriage market. Parents try to ensure that theirs is the best possible proposition. Originally, the idea of the dowry system had some merit, in that it was supposed to provide the woman with some money of her own: as she could not inherit property, she was given the next best thing – money, *her* money, her only form of independence.

Nowadays, the principle has been turned on its head. The dowry is paid straight to the husband's family and the bride is unlikely to see any of it. Worse than this, however, is the horrible phenomenon, now so common in India, of 'dowry deaths', whereby wives are killed by their husbands' families because the dowry has not been what was promised, or what was expected. It was recently reported that brides had been killed in this way because a promised motor scooter or hi-fi had not materialized. In one month, an estimated 400 dowry deaths took place in the Bombay area – and all for tiny amounts of money or trivial consumer items. The stranglehold of the dowry system has meant that families wishing to get their daughters married off (and in India, remember, an unmarried daughter in the family is considered a disgrace) often pretend to greater riches than they actually possess.

The tradition of arranged marriages is in itself causing untold misery among Indians nowadays. Those in favour of arranged marriages claim that they are just as likely to be long-lasting and happy as those in which two young people have freely come together out of mutual love and regard. Indian arranged marriages are celebrated with, if anything, even greater ritual and ceremony than is common in Western countries; such marriages are big events in a family's life. In India, as in other Eastern countries, there is the sense that two families are marrying, not merely two individuals, which would perhaps seem to make a grand ceremony even more necessary in the cause of strengthening those bonds.

This was certainly the case for Benazir Bhutto, the attractive – and in many ways very Westernized – daughter of the former president of Pakistan who is now leader of her country's opposition government. After years of being a bachelor girl she announced that she was to marry, and that the marriage had been arranged by her family. It is unlikely, however, that Benazir will be a traditional wife. Announcing her engagement to Asif Zardari, from one of the richest families in Pakistan, she said, in a statement that highlighted a total reversal of the usual marital situation: 'I don't want a husband who is involved in politics and I certainly don't want to come home to discuss politics. I want a husband with interests of his own and his own career.' Benazir also pledged that she would not be giving up her political activities because of marriage.

Until recently most Indians have stayed silent on their custom of arranged marriage. But now that many live in Western countries and are having to try to reconcile their own traditions with those of an alien and rather hostile culture, more are speaking out.

One is Sharan-Jeet Shah, author of *In My Own Name*. Interviewed about marriage, Sikh-style, she said:

My book is not a diatribe against arranged marriages. Indeed, I am certain that when a marriage is arranged with the complete consent of both partners and a thorough appraisal of each other's backgrounds, it stands a very good chance of success, maybe even a better chance than 'love marriages'. But for me the arranged marriage system wrecked my life and it has taken me twenty years to pick up the pieces and carve out a successful career.

She spoke of the terrible dilemmas faced by Eastern women who want to marry the man of their choice. They risk ostracism, humiliation and being put on to the streets, destitute. It is odd that marriage, which is supposed to be such a joyful occasion, should so often be the cause of enormous dissension. Parents may say they want their children to be happy, but what they really want to achieve is conformity and the outward appearance of everything being done properly. This is even more true of Eastern countries than it is of the West, where children carry far less of a burden of 'respect' whether deserved or not, to their elders, and can defy their parents without incurring retribution of a catastrophic order.

In Sharan-Jeet's case, her nightmare began when she secretly married a Muslim student while she was at medical school. As soon as her father found out about the marriage, he removed her from medical school, locked her up and made her divorce her husband to marry instead a man chosen for her: a 30-year-old stranger who was uneducated and desperately in debt. Her new husband, by law, now owned her. 'He was second to God in my life,' she explains. 'I was expected to serve and obey and never defend myself verbally. Though I let him claim his conjugal rights, I would freeze, close my eyes tight and pray for those moments to be over as quickly as possible. Afterwards I wanted to be sick.'

Eventually she gained the strength to leave him and to qualify as a teacher, bringing up her two sons on her own. However, her independent action cost her the love of her family, who no longer speak to her.

In the West we tend to regard arranged marriages as barbaric. Yet Western marriages are in some respects almost as much arranged. It is very rare, after all, for people to marry outside their class and type. When they do, there is always a lot of fuss, as there was *à propos* of the wedding of Edward VIII to Mrs Simpson. He was giving up a throne to marry the woman he loved – and for this he was sent into exile. Although marriage is supposed to be for love, there is patently much more to it than that. Almost all marriages are marriages of 'convenience' of one sort or another, and the 'love' is often just a degraded, sentimental version of the real thing.

A report by Professor Neville Butler of Bristol University, who is carrying out a major study of child and teenage behaviour, revealed that by far the great majority of young people do not marry for love. Instead, they marry to escape their families, because they fear loneliness, or because they want to seem adult. Very rarely is there overwhelming love for the marriage partner.

This was made clear to me when I was teaching in a girls' grammar school in the North East of England where, at the time, at least half of the staff seemed to be getting married. Every day they would talk excitedly about their dress, shoes, 'something old, something new', the reception – yet hardly ever did they mention the men they were going to marry. They were so caught up in the ritual that the man had become almost incidental. It was as if almost anybody would have done. Many young women still marry more because they want to be married, and thereby escape families, loneliness and the last vestiges of childhood, than because they have fallen deeply in love. They like the idea of a wedding, setting up home, being grown up (if you have spent all your previous years as a child living in your parents' home, this can be very appealing), but it never crosses their minds that every traditional wedding that takes place helps to perpetuate a male-dominated society.

Even people who opt for simple registry-office weddings are doing this. At the time of getting married, the more far-sighted of brides may feel that giving up their independence will not matter because the couple's love for each other will make this pale into insignificance. But after a few years it will, and the constant togetherness is likely to become very irksome: so much for the fantasy that marriage will bring happiness.

Weddings are a displacement activity which serves to make people forget about the resentment and hostility which will almost inevitably set in once the ceremony is over. Many people experience great disappointment when they discover that the person they married is not the dream companion or Prince Charming they had hoped for but just a rather boring and ordinary human being; yet surely we must realize that the world is full of unremarkable people, and we are likely to be marrying one of them.

We try to make our chosen partner seem special for this one day, even if we know that he or she is not special, and that the reasons for our marriage are not all that special either.

If marriage as a legal entity were abolished, weddings would no longer take place and the wedding industry would collapse. But, you may ask, wouldn't life be sadder and greyer without weddings? How could anybody be such a killjoy as to want to outlaw them?

I would agree – if statistics suggested that marriage was good for us or that it could be shown to increase the sum of human happiness. But no one could claim this. The average Western marriage now lasts nine years, and its end is normally marked by intense acrimony and hostility. It is estimated that at least 50 per cent of husbands have extra-marital affairs. No ceremony in the world can stop this happening. It is also estimated that cystitis (formerly known as 'honeymoon cystitis') is now reaching epidemic proportions among women who are sexually active.

Unholy Matrimony

Misery of one kind or another sets in all too soon after the wedding. The lavishness of the ceremony may even serve to increase the eventual misery. People think that, having gone through so much, and after so much money has been spent, they have every right to be happy and they feel guilty for not being so: after all, lots of wellwishers took trouble to wish them future happiness, even took part in a religious service in order to do so, then shared a banquet with them and toasted them. Surely all this meant they could expect to be happy?

The conventions and customs surrounding weddings and marriages are very powerful. Only with a complete change of consciousness throughout society could the status quo be shaken. All the laws and ceremonies of marriage have been established by men – and women have acquiesced, even taking over the practical arrangements in the belief that, for a girl, the day she gets married is her 'big day'. Thereafter her achievements will be limited, in all likelihood, to what she can fit in when she is not busy 'supporting' her husband.

Not so long ago the American magazine *Mad* carried a cartoon of a mother weeping at a ceremony where her clever daughter was having yet another impressive degree conferred on her.

'What's the matter?' a friend is asking her. 'Your daughter's a qualified doctor, she's a psychiatrist, head of her department... What are you upset about?'

'She's not married yet,' the mother wails.

This joke was funny to readers because we all understand that, whatever other successes a girl may achieve, marriage still constitutes the ultimate success – even though it is something so common and ordinary that it is within virtually everybody's grasp.

Many mothers of the bride do not like to feel they have been 'cheated' out of arranging and attending a big ceremony for their daughters. Often their daughters claim that they go along with it just to please their mothers. In turn they will do the same thing with their own daughters.

Yet there is no doubt that weddings are a strain, and the smiles of the key participants in the photographs only thinly mask this.

Even the guest list usually serves to offend or upset some people (as in all the fairy stories in which the uninvited guest wreaks a terrible vengeance at a later date), and long-dormant family feuds often rise to the surface again when weddings are being planned.

Would society really be any the poorer if there were no more lavish weddings, and if people remained eternally single in law, having their unions blessed in a place of worship only if they so desired? Surely, on the contrary, everybody would be a whole lot better off – with the sole exception, perhaps, of those whose livelihood is derived from arranging weddings.

10

Credo

Anybody who has persevered with this book thus far will have gathered that marriage is, to my mind, a completely outdated, irrelevant and inappropriate institution in the context of today's society. The traditional idea of marriage is no more than patriarchalism asserting itself, and reaffirming the superiority of men over women, without offering any reasons why the male sex should be so regarded. The phrase 'holy matrimony' tries to persuade us that the concept is enshrined in holy writ, that it was God who ordained that men should have authority over women. But because the aura of fantasy surrounding marriage, and particularly weddings, is so overwhelming, we tend not to recognize the insidious damage that the institution inflicts upon women: 'O perfect love, all human thought transcending' (the first line of a popular Church of England wedding hymn) has an ironic, even cynical, undertone that reflects the swamping of reality by fantasy hopes and sentiments. It was years before I realized it myself: high-flown sentiments are consummately effective in the role of shrouding unpalatable truths.

Like so many other young women, when I married I blithely went along with all the conventions: changing my name, calling myself 'Mrs' and obliterating myself in all kinds of ways, from not having my own motor insurance to not having my own name in the telephone directory, and by changing my name on my passport, driving licence and all other personal documents. Indeed, even as short a time ago as the mid-1960s, it was considered that to change from 'Miss' to 'Mrs' was a form of upgrading for a woman. I even acquiesced, for a time, to the tradition of wearing a wedding ring – the supreme symbol of bondage.

Now that I have come to understand what the state of marriage

Unholy Matrimony

really means, the logic behind my call for its abolition seems to me irrefutable. So why should my views seem so radical? Why do so many politicians (and not only male ones) still want to 'honour' marriage? Why do so many middle-aged women still look forward with joy to their daughters' weddings and regard them as the 'big day' of these young women's lives?

Why do so many women who get divorced rush into remarriage so quickly? Why do so many women unthinkingly accept the humiliating custom of calling themselves by their husbands' names ('Mrs John Smith') and behave as though their husbands are far more important than they are?

Modern marriage is not, after all, a resounding success: more than one in three fails, and the average duration of marriages in Europe and America is now only nine years. The vast number of letters received by newspaper and magazine advice columnists, the number of couples who consult marriage guidance counsellors and the number of women, in particular, who resort to tranquillizers to try to obliterate their marital unhappiness suggest that a vast proportion of those who marry experience major problems and emotional trauma in the pursuit of marital bliss.

I believe that there are two main reasons why we persist in getting married – against all the odds and against all the evidence that our happiness will be augmented by it. Even though so many more people are now 'cohabiting', state-instituted marriage is still seen as the norm and many couples who cohabit for a time eventually marry. Even avowed feminists sometimes get married, in the assumption that this is the best, indeed the only, way of making a binding commitment to their partners. Few of us ever ask ourselves whether it is a good idea to make such a commitment, or whether such 'commitment' is indeed possible, or desirable. There is a reference in the popular hymn mentioned earlier to those 'whom Thou for evermore dost join in one'. Marriage tries to turn two individuals into one; if they merely cohabit, they remain separate beings. Yet the 'one flesh' concept obviously has a great appeal for very many people: they genuinely long for total togetherness.

Credo

One important reason why so many people still marry is that human beings are, above all, creatures of habit. Most of us hate to deviate in any significant way from what other people do. The majority of us have grown up with the idea that marriage is one of life's great events, much like being born or dying. In fact, for women in some cultures, marriage is seen as a rebirth. In India women change not only their last but also their first names, and in Japan they wear different clothes to signify their married status. Even in the West we acknowledge a change of status and of objectives and expectations when a woman marries. This is not, however, our reason for marrying. Ultimately, most of us get married simply because everybody around us seems to be doing it, and we do not want to be any different. Even in the late 1980s men and women who do not marry – unless they are professed gays or lesbians – are considered slightly odd. Habits, good *or* bad, are very hard to break. People often remarry after one marriage breaks down simply because they have got into the habit of being married and cannot see any other way of conducting their lives.

The other fundamental reason for marriage is that human beings are gregarious creatures, and their desire for constant companionship runs very deep. Few of us want to walk through life alone, and few of us have the strength to do so. We imagine that we will find this companionship in an intimate, exclusive and long-lasting union with one member of the opposite sex. The idea of the 'couple', so prevalent in our society today, is to safeguard against the terrible loneliness which many imagine will descend upon them if they do not enter into a legally-binding union which will confer mutual possession as well as permanently altering their status and position in law.

The fact that it is easy to be just as lonely within wedlock as outside it seems to occur to very few individuals indeed.

My argument against marriage is not against companionship, friendship and rapport with others. Few of us, after all, want to be hermits; but marriage is no guarantee of friendship or companionship. Indeed, as my brief historical survey of marriage revealed, the idea that it should be companionate came very late in the institution's history, and because it was originally formulated to protect property and inheritance this makes it very hard for marital partners to be friends. When we are bound together in a too-close, cloying relationship, it becomes very easy for love to turn to hate. Yet, even when hate has replaced love, there is still deep attachment, as demonstrated in the stories of spouses killing, or attempting to kill, their partners, either because they no longer pleased or because they had fallen in love with another. Such attachment is not therefore very desirable or healthy. After all, if a friend of ours were to find another friend, we would not normally wish to bump our friend off. When we become so bound up with another person, especially someone of the opposite sex, it is likely that in time highly negative emotions will set in. Sex is a contributory factor, because the expectations on the part of two disparate individuals can never be the same. Where the relationship is non-sexual, this source of irritation and disappointment is not a factor.

All the problems within marriage arise, I believe, through the idea that we own our partners. 'Commitment', which leads people to marry rather than merely to cohabit, has at its root the concept of possession. When we marry somebody, we are saying to the world at large: this is mine – hands off.

It is very pleasant, indeed life-enhancing, to have close friends; companionship makes all events more enjoyable. Unfortunately, the institution of marriage serves to militate against friendship. We do not, on the whole, form indissoluble legally enforceable bonds with our friends. Indeed, one of the reasons why people tend to remain friends is that they are detached from each other. It is very difficult to have a proper friendship with somebody who is yoked to you by law – and with whom you cannot have the kind of relationship you might desire.

Once you enter into marriage, your legal status is altered whether you like it or not, and whether or not you agree with it. If you have made a will, it will be presumed to be revoked. If you are a woman, your legal position will be diminished; if you are a man it will be enhanced. Married men instantly become entitled to state benefits which are denied to single men, yet married women have their benefits taken away. As a married person you will be expected, in society as in law, to operate as a pair, not as one of two individuals, and will be considered odd if you do not. A recent interview with Sarah Lawson, wife of Michael Grade, the head of Channel Four Television, referred to the 'bizarre marriage' of this couple, who spend several months of each year apart on different continents. You are also considered odd if your marital relationship does not include regular sex (as I know from experience) and if you decide to live apart despite being on good terms with your partner. The writer Vera Brittain was thought to be very strange because her great friend the novelist Winifred Holtby continued to live with her after Vera married George Catlin.

Marriage imposes enormous restraints on our behaviour and leaves very little room for manoeuvre.

In the days when marriage existed principally to protect property and inheritance, there was some point to the institution. Nowadays the importance of the family has declined. It may still be the basic social unit, but families no longer wage wars on one another and few people outside royal and aristocratic circles care about dynasties any more. Hereditary positions of power have almost vanished and with them the need for families, and for sons to protect territories.

Many people who are not married, or who have left behind an unsatisfactory marriage, discover to their delight that they can have more friends and acquaintances and be far freer in their relationships than when they are yoked into a constraining, intimate union. To be unmarried does not necessarily mean that a person will be lonely, or even alone.

The abolition of marriage would mean that many different kinds of union could be recognized. At present, society is uneasy about same-sex unions, even though these are often much closer and more harmonious than opposite-sex ones. Such relationships are still seen as 'unnatural'. In the past, the main reason was because they were sterile. Now, single women and lesbian couples have children by alternative insemination, and although men cannot as yet bear children, the time when this *is* technically possible may not be all that far off. (This sounds weird and perhaps distasteful, but only ten years ago test-tube babies sounded like something from science fiction: now they are an everyday reality, as are surrogate mothers.) For all these reasons, the distinctions between legitimate and illegitimate children have become nonsensical. Now that eggs and sperm can be donated, frozen, activated with machines and chemicals, the idea of preserving family lines and family names is no longer relevant.

Whether or not one wishes to regard children as a necessary adjunct to adulthood, the fact remains that many people are finding their own alternatives to marriage, with or without legislation. In the UK the trend against marriage, according to a survey published in the *Daily Express* (December 1987), is most marked in women aged 25 to 34. Three out of four of those who took part had decided to set up home with their boyfriends without getting married. So although few people are vociferously calling for the abolition of marriage, ever more are voting with their feet by deciding not to change their single status.

In other countries, the trend against marriage is even more marked. But the fact that people are not getting married does not mean they are living alone. By far the great majority of unmarried people under 40 are in steady relationships. According to the same survey reported in the *Daily Express*, elderly women comprise the main group of people who live alone, and in most cases these are probably widows.

Those who choose to cohabit will find, before long, that a set of laws very similar to those governing marriage has been devised, to give cohabitees the same types of claim on each other as married couples – simply because they have lived together or shared a home for a time. The qualifying factor for the 'cohabitation' label is sexual intercourse: this alone can grant one person rights to another's possessions. Mistresses may now claim for a proportion of their former lovers' homes and incomes when their relationships end. This principle, established in 1977 in the USA and known as 'palimony', began when a judge awarded a sum of money to the former mistress of the actor Lee Marvin, who claimed in court that she had given him, besides sex, the 'best years of her life', as well as abandoning her career in order to further his. Although the monetary award was nominal, a precedent was established that even those who live together outside wedlock may have claims on each other, as long as they have been having sexual intercourse.

Women, unfortunately, still cleave to an inferior role, whether they are married or merely cohabiting. All too many, even nowadays, give up their independent incomes and careers to serve men. And possessiveness, too, is till rife: men think they own their wives, and women think they own their husbands. Abolition of marriage would enable women to relate to men in a freer and more equal way. Indeed, it could be the greatest advance in the emancipation of women since, seven decades ago, they were at last given the vote.

I believe we hang on to the idea of marriage, of 'perfect love', out of sentiment and fear – fear of change. We should now be happy to let this irrelevant institution slip into the pages of history and work instead to develop the autonomy and independence of the individual. Friendship and companionship, which genuinely enhance life, should be our alternative goal.

Bibliography

Ardener, Shirley, and Callan, Hilary: *The Incorporated Wife* (Croom Helm, 1984)
Armstrong, Karen: *The Gospel According To Woman* (Pan, 1987)
Austen, Jane: *Pride and Prejudice* (Penguin Classics, 1986)
Ayckbourn, Alan: *Woman in Mind* (play, first produced 1987; published by Samuel French, 1987)

Bernard, Jessie: *The Future of Marriage* (Souvenir, 1973)
Book of Common Prayer (Oxford University Press)
Bosch, Susanne: *Jenny Lives with Eric and Martin* (Gay Men's Press, 1986)
Botham, Kathy: *Living with a Legend* (Grafton, 1987)
Bottomley, Anne; Gieve, Katherine; Moon, Gay; Weir, Angela: *The Cohabitation Handbook: a woman's guide to the law* (Pluto Press, 1984)
Braine, John: *Room at the Top* (Penguin, 1957)

Daly, Mary: *Gyn/Ecology* (The Women's Press, 1984)
Dante: *The Divine Comedy*, translated by Dorothy L. Sayers (Penguin, 1966)
Donne, John: *Collected Poems* (Oxford University Press, 1933)

Foot, Paul: *Red Shelley* (Sidgwick and Jackson, 1980)
Freedman, Michael D.A. and Lyon, Christina M.: *Cohabitation Without Marriage* (Gower, 1982)
French, Marilyn: *Beyond Power: Men, Women and Morals* (Jonathan Cape, 1985)

Garnett, Angelica: *Deceived with Kindness* (Chatto and Windus, 1984)
Goldsmith, Oliver: *She Stoops to Conquer* (1773)
Greer, Germaine: *Sex and Destiny* (Secker and Warburg, 1984)

Haldane, Charlotte: *Motherhood and Its Enemies* (Chatto, 1927)
Hamilton, Cicely: *Marriage as a Trade* (The Women's Press, 1981)
Hendry, Joy: *Marriage in Changing Japan* (Croom Helm, 1981)

Jeffreys, Sheila: *The Spinster and Her Enemies, Feminism and Sexuality, 1880-1930* (Pandora, 1985)
Jowell, Roger; Witherstone, Sharon and Brook, Lindsay (editors): *British Social Attitudes: social and community planning research* (Gower, 1987)

Mill, J.S.: *The Subjection of Women* (Everyman's Library, Dent, 1970)
Mitteraner, Michael, and Reinhard, Sieder: *The European Family* (Basil Blackwell, 1982)

Oakley, Ann: *Taking It Like a Woman* (Flamingo, 1985)

Rubin, Lilian: *Intimate Strangers: what goes wrong in relationships today and why* (Fontana, 1983)

Sadat, Jehan: *A Woman of Egypt* (Bloomsbury, 1987)
Shah, Sharan-Jeet: *In My Own Name* (The Women's Press, 1987)
Steinem, Gloria: *Outrageous Acts and Everyday Rebellions* (Flamingo, 1984)
Stone, Lawrence: *The Family, Sex and Marriage in England, 1500-1800* (Weidenfeld and Nicolson, 1977)

Tawney, R.H.: *Religion and the Rise of Capitalism* (Pelican, 1961)

Vaughan, Diane: *Uncoupling* (Methuen, 1987)

Wollstonecraft, Mary: *A Vindication of the Rights of Woman* (Pelican 1985)
Women: a World Report (Methuen, 1985)
Woolf, Virginia: *A Room of One's Own* (Granada, 1983)
Woolf, Virginia: *Three Guineas* (Granada, 1983)

Index

affairs, extra-marital, 42-3, 130, 132, 191
AID (Artificial Insemination by Donor), 169, 170-1, 199
AIDS, 24, 28, 116
alimony, 15
Anne, Princess, 35, 95
Aquino, Corazon, 86
Archer, Jeffrey, 26-8
Archer, Mary, 26-8, 33
Ardener, Shirley, 112
Aristophanes, 77
Armstrong, Karen, 57, 118-19, 120
Ashbrook, David, 37
Astell, Mary, 92-3
Austen, Jane, 73
Australia, 15, 152
Ayckbourn, Alan, 94

bachelors, 123, 135-6
Bandaranaike, Mrs, 86
Barber, Janet, 39
Beeston, Michael, 41
Bernard, Jessie, 91, 93, 103-8
Besley, Caroline, 41
Beveridge, William, 143
Bhutto, Benazir, 13, 188-9
Body Shop, The, 80
Botham, Ian, 89
Botham, Kathy, 89
Boyce, Christabel, 36
Boyce, Nicholas, 35-6
Brophy, Brigid, 168-9
Buckley, Christine, 37
Buckley, William, 37
Braine, John, 132
breadwinners, 16, 31, 44, 148, 149, 165, 169

Brittain, Vera, 199
Butler, Professor Neville, 190
Byron, George Gordon, Lord, 130

Callan, Hilary, 112
Canada, 15
Cartland, Barbara, 150
Catlin, George, 199
celibacy, 54, 118, 119, 123
Centre for Economic Policy Research, 133
Chapone, Hester, 93
Charles, Prince, *see* Wales, Prince of
child benefit, 114, 146, 155, 156, 166
childbirth, 81-2, 98, 133, 176, 199-200
children, 10, 12, 34-5, 49, 64, 66, 102-3, 124, 125, 129, 157-79
Christianity, 117, 118-23, 157, 181
Chudleigh, Lady, 92
Church of England, 11
Civil Evidence Act 1968, 18
Coghlan, Monica, 26
cohabitation, 141-5, 150-3, 166-7, 174, 196, 198, 200-1
commitment, 9, 10, 24, 28, 43, 108, 179, 198
companionship, 9, 10, 13, 17, 19, 197, 198
computer dating, 78
Congreve, William, 57
consortium, 18
contraception, 91, 177
contract (of marriage), 11, 12, 15, 53, 145, 146, 153, 178-9
Corlett, Erika, 36-7
Corlett, Thomas, 36-7
Council of Trent, 48
crime, domestic, 35-42

Crippen, Dr Hawley Harvey, 36
cystitis, 191

Daly, Mary, 110, 183
Dallas (television serial), 63
Dante Alighieri, 50
Davies, Dr Brenda, 38
depression, 23, 104
Dickens, Frank, 135
Diplomatic Service Wives' Association, 112
divorce, 10, 11, 15, 18, 20, 24, 30, 48, 52, 62, 80, 81, 108, 153, 177-8, 182
Donne, John, 50
dowries, 49, 187-8
Drabble, Margaret, 18
Dynasty (television serial), 63

Edward VIII, 185, 190
Edwards, Linda, 170-1
Elberskircher, Joanna, 100
Ellis, Havelock, 99
Equal Pay Act, 149

families, 49-50, 53, 63, 119-20, 126, 162-3, 199
family income supplement, 16, 144
family law, 144
Family Law Reform Act, 173
Family Psychicenter, St Louis, 135
Family Policy Studies Centre, 133
family rooms (in hospitals), 82
fidelity, 27, 28, 30, 33
Fiennes, Sir Ranulph, 75
Foot, Paul, 127, 128
Foreign Office, 111-12
Freedman, Michael, 142-5, 147, 150-1
French, Mr Justice, 138
French, Marilyn, 130, 177
French Revolution, 128
friendship, 9, 197, 198, 201

Garner, Lesley, 45
Garnett, Angelica, 46
Garnett, 'Bunny', 46
Godwin, William, 59, 128
Goldsmith, Oliver, 73
Gorbachev, Raisa, 84, 86
Grade, Michael, 199
Greene, Graham, 18
Greer, Germaine, 21, 85, 87, 177
Gwalior, Maharajah of, 187

Hadjipateras, Angela, 173
Hadley, Katharine, 89
Haldane, Charlotte, 99
Hamilton, Cicely, 95-8
Hanbury-Tenison, Robin, 75
happiness, 21, 23
Hart, Gary, 25
Healey, Robert, 39
Heath, Edward, 75
Hendry, Joy, 68-71
Henpecked Husbands Society, 134
Hewitt, Patricia, 141
Hitler, Adolf, 176
Hockestra, Mrs, 186
Hockestra, Tami, 186
Hogg, Sarah, 140
Holroyd, Michael, 18
Holtby, Winifred, 199
homosexuality, 13, 29, 86, 116, 130, 132-3, 169-70, 197
honeymoons, 29, 187, 191
housekeeping, 19
housework, 106
Huffington, Michael, 186

illegitimacy, 17, 115, 146, 151, 167-8, 171-3, 178, 200
Imlay, Gilbert, 59
immigration, 14
impotence, 12
infertility, 176
intimacy, 21, 64, 73-4, 77-8, 79-80, 144

Jeffreys, Sheila, 99-101
Jesus Christ, 118-19, 168
Joannou, Marion, 42
Joannou, Michael, 42
John, Elton, 89
Julian of Norwich, 124

Keating, Alistair, 36
Keating, Margaret, 36
Keays, Sara, 25
Keeler, Christine, 25
Kenny, Mary, 74-5
kibbutzim, 174
Kinnock, Glenys, 84
Kinnock, Neil, 84
Kirkman, Raymond, 38, 39
Kirkman, Sandy, 38-9
Koestler, Arthur, 23

Koestler, Cynthia, 23
Kraty, Janet, 41
Kraty, Nigel, 41
Kyte, Diana, 40

Ladakh, 47
Lambton, Lord, 25
Laura Ashley plc, 80
Lawson, Sarah, 199
'learned helplessness', 22
Lee-Potter, Lynda, 28
legal status, 9, 14, 15, 16, 20, 94, 104, 141, 146, 198
lesbians, 29, 86, 99, 102, 116, 133, 152, 169, 177, 199
loneliness, 10, 197
Lord Hardwicke's Act, 53, 139
love, 9, 11, 13, 26, 29, 30, 31, 33, 42, 43, 49, 50, 51, 54, 56, 58, 59, 98, 102, 108, 109-10; and honour, 14, 15, 21, 54
Lucan, Lord, 36
Lyon, Christina, 142-5, 147, 150-1

maintenance, 15, 144, 151, 178
Malthus, 127
marriage, in Africa, 48; arranged, 13, 62, 187-90; bureaux, 78; in church, 52-6; consummation, 12; of convenience, 14; and crime, 35-42; duration in West, 191; and financial security, 34; in Europe, 50, 63-7; in history, 47-71; in India, 67, 79-80; 187-90, 197; in Japan, 68-71, 186-7, 197; and the law, 139-156; and men, 48-9, 104-5, 117-37; monogamy, 129, 144; open, 12, 74, 130; as patriarchal institution, 16, 48, 99, 100, 117, 195; polyandry, 47; polygamy, 11, 47; qualifications for, 11; and sex, 11-12, 13, 24-6, 29, 33, 48-9, 51-2, 94, 99, 100, 121, 130; and women, 17, 44-5, 55-8, 91-116; vows, 14, 15, 54-5, 184
married man's allowance, 16
Married Women's Property Act, 19, 100
Marvin, Lee, 200
Mary Queen of Scots, 57
Mason, Helen, 27-8
matrimonial home, 17, 19, 42-3
Matrimonial Homes Act, 19

Mediation in Divorce Conciliation Service, 10
Mill, John Stuart, 94
Millett, Kate, 142
Mitford, Nancy, 158
Muggeridge, Kitty, 23
Muggeridge, Malcolm, 23
Murphy, Dervla, 75
Muslim societies, 21, 118

National Children's Bureau, 160
National Children's Home, 163
National Marriage Guidance Council (Relate), 51
Nightingale, Florence, 99

Oakley, Ann, 94, 108-10
Odent, Dr Michel, 82
Office of Population, Census and Surveys, 10
One-Parent Families, National Council for, 167, 173
Osborn, Rev. David, 36
Owen, Deborah, 84

'palimony', 200-1
Pankhurst, Christabel, 99
Parkinson, Cecil, 25
pensions, 154-5
Philip, Prince, 85
Pithers, David, 163
Plimmer, Martin, 136-7
poll tax, 145
poison (as agent of murder), 39
Profumo, John, 25
property (marriages as transfer of), 17, 19-20, 144, 184, 198, 199

Quiller, David, 41
Quiller, Yvonne, 41

Rajneesh, Shree Bhagwan, 44
rape (in marriage), 18
Reagan, Nancy, 84, 86, 186
Reformation, 11, 53, 118, 123, 124
reproduction, 11, 12, 47, 49
Ridley, Patrick, 134
rituals, 48, 181-93
Rocha, Juan, 186
Rochefoucauld, Duc de, 60
Royal, The Princess, *see* Anne, Princess
Rubin, Lilian, 147

Unholy Matrimony

rule of thumb, 51

Sadat, Anwar, 84
Sadat, Jehan, 84, 86
St Paul, 119
Savvides, Angelo, 38
Savvides, Helena, 38
Scandinavia (marriage laws), 143, 144-5, 150
Sex Discrimination Act, 154
Sex Reform Congress, 100
Shah, Sharan-Jeet, 189-90
Shelley, Mary, 58, 126-7
Shelley, Percy Bysshe, 58, 126-9, 148, 156, 166
Simpson, Wallis (Duchess of Windsor), 185, 190
singles bars, 77
singles holidays, 77
Snowdon, Dr Robert, 102-3
Spencer, Lady Diana, 14, 61-2
sperm banks, 102
spinsters, 58, 95, 99, 100, 123
'spousals', 53
Stassinopoulos, Arianna, 186
Steel, Judy, 84
Steinem, Gloria, 86
Stephenson, Robert, 41
Stone, Lawrence, 50-1, 93, 94
Stopes, Marie, 100
Stoppard, Dr Miriam, 83
Stoppard, Tom, 83
supplementary benefit, 16, 143
surnames, 166-7
surrogate mothers, 200

Tawney, R. H., 123
taxation, 139, 140-1
Taylor, Greg, 40
Thatcher, Denis, 84, 85, 89
Thatcher, Margaret, 25, 95
togetherness, 21, 24, 73-90
Townend, Peter, 95
tranquillizers, 77, 105, 196

Wages for Housework Campaign, 148
Wales, Prince of, 14, 61-2, 74
Wales, Princess of, 14, 61-2, 74
Walker, Ian, 40
Walker, Rosemary, 40
Walton, John, 41
Watkins, John, 39
Watkins, Margaret, 39
weddings, 181-93
Westbrook, Harriet (first Mrs Shelley), 58, 126
widows, 143
wife, dependent, 44, 88, 121, 129, 139, 142-3, 144, 154, 164; incorporated, 87, 110-13
wills, 19-20, 146, 151
Windsor, House of, 14
Woolf, Virginia, 97
Wollstonecraft, Mary, 58, 59, 128-9

'urge to merge', 22-3

Vaughan, Diane, 78, 79
virginity, 12, 185

Zajonc, Robert, 22